Understanding Nervousness
in
Horse and Rider

Understanding Nervousness
in
Horse and Rider

Moyra Williams

J. A. Allen
London

British Library Cataloguing in Publication Data
Williams, Moyra
    Understanding nervousness in horse and rider.
    1. Livestock: Horses. Training
    I. Title
    636.1083

    Cased edition: ISBN 0–85131–530–5
    Paperback edition: ISBN 0–85131–501–1

Published in Great Britain in 1990 by
J. A. Allen & Company Limited
1 Lower Grosvenor Place
London SW1W 0EL

Reprinted 1994, 1995

© J. A. Allen & Company Limited 1990

Book production Bill Ireson
Typeset by Fakenham Photosetting Limited, Fakenham, Norfolk
Printed in Hong Kong

Acknowledgements

I am greatly indebted to all those who have helped me by providing information that is included in this book, especially Sabrina Benson, Jeremy Bramham Law, T. P. Ryan FWCF, Lesley Young (BHSAI), for her contribution on teaching, and all the members of the Equine Behaviour Study Circle.

I am also most grateful to J. A. Davies for permission to reprint his lovely poem from *The Reins of Life*. My thanks also to Anne Pilgrim, who drew the cartoons.

Contents

List of Illustrations

Introduction

Apart from the dog, there is probably no species of animal with which people have shared life longer or in more varied ways than the horse. Archaeological traces and historical records show that these two species seem to have lived happily alongside one another since their ancestors first appeared on earth.

Not only is the length of their association remarkable, but its breadth, or range, is also probably unique. There is hardly a branch of human activity in which we have not enlisted the aid of this quadruped, for example, transport, agriculture, battle, ceremony, art and competition.

Despite this length of association, there is still much that can be learned about the horse. As the world changes, so do the problems that have to be faced by those who live in it, both equine and human. I have long been fascinated by the manner in which the horses and humans of today try to solve their problems, and in 1976 I helped to set up a competition to look deeper into the matter. The variety of suggestions received, the fields that different people studied, and the ways in which these studies were carried out indicated that many other people were as interested in this area as I was.

In 1978, Gillian Cooper – a long-time student of the horse and a well-known writer under the pen-name of Susan McBane – suggested that a group be formed – the Equine Behaviour Study Circle (EBSC) – through which members from all parts of the world could communicate with one another via a bi-annual newsletter, *Equine Behaviour*. The circle thrived and has been active ever since; much of the content of the following pages is taken from various numbers of *Equine Behaviour*.

The stories these writers tell, and the way in which they tell them, may not seem very impressive to people who still feel (as I was taught to do when first studying science in the mid-1950s) that every observation is valueless unless backed by statistics based on many cases. In recent years, however, 'single-case studies' have become acceptable again, especially in the solution of psychological problems, and nervousness is certainly one of these – perhaps the commonest of them all. It can affect all creatures in all situations, and overcoming nervousness can still provide one of the greatest senses of achievement.

How is it overcome? The first essential is to be able to recognise its presence. This might seem ridiculous but the fact remains that an individual can suffer a great deal of misery by refusing to admit that he is afraid of a situation (and thereby inviting ridicule from his fellows), or by failing to realise that the agony he is experiencing from cramped muscles or sensory lapses is due to fear or nervousness.

The second essential is to know the steps by which nervousness may be overcome. The simplest, of course, is removal of the cause, but this may not always be practical as it may lead to a severe restriction of habitat or activity, or to a general decrease in living standards. Various ways in which nervousness *can* be overcome – and the action that the sufferer needs to take to do so – are nowadays fairly well understood, and can be followed by any individual.

The third essential – and perhaps the least well understood – is to be aware of all the situations that may lead to nervousness. These vary not only between the different animal species, but also between different individuals of the same species. No two horses are alike just as no two people are alike. Nevertheless, all living creatures have certain features in common and will react to some situations in more or less the same way.

Nothing contained within the following pages is entirely

new, or was unknown to the specialist before publication, but all too frequently old truths tend to be forgotten – or fail to be handed on from one generation to another – and it is to prevent this happening to the modern horse and its rider or handler that this book has been written.

PART I

The Nature of Nervousness

CHAPTER I

What is Nervousness?

'If we had to choose just one quality which, in essence, describes the mentality or temperament of the horse family, I think it would have to be nervousness', wrote Susan McBane in *Behaviour Problems in Horses*. But what is nervousness?

The word 'nervous' has many definitions. *Black's Veterinary Dictionary* (13th edition, published 1979) does not mention the word; nor does *Harrap's Dictionary of Current English Usage – Word Perfect* (1978). *Longman's Modern English Dictionary* (1976) and the Clarendon Press's *Shorter Oxford English Dictionary* (1987), on the other hand, give a variety of definitions including 'self-consciousness', 'lacking confidence', 'suffering from disorders of the central nervous system', 'excitable', 'easily agitated and apprehensive'; while *Summerhays's Encyclopaedia for Horsemen* (4th edition, 1952) says nerve is 'Courage in the hunting field – the reverse of nerves'. Naturally, these definitions are mostly intended to refer to people.

The point that Summerhays makes seems to me particularly important, and shows how many English words can vary in their meaning according to their context. The word 'nerve' in the context 'You've got a nerve' means something quite different from the same word in the sense 'He's all nerves'. In the same way, 'nervous', when referring to fear or apprehension, means something quite different when referring to excitement. Not only are the sensations accompanying the former unpleasant while those accompanying the latter are often very enjoyable, they can also have totally opposite effects on the body.

The nervous system has its headquarters in the brain. Messages from the different sense organs (eyes, ears, nose, mouth, skin, etc.), arrive in the brain via the central nervous system. The brain co-ordinates them with messages from the rest of the body (including the heart, lungs, glands, etc.) and with memories from the past, and sends out appropriate orders to the muscles. The responses of the muscles will be largely influenced by chemicals liberated into the bloodstream by the glands as a result of the reaction and by memories evoked in the brain.

If the incoming message has been associated with something pleasant in the past, the chemicals liberated by the brain will deactivate the nerves and so relax the muscles; but if it was associated with something unpleasant, the chemicals will keep the nervous energy flowing and the muscles tight and ready for action.

The great danger with an unpleasant, fear-provoking stimulus, is that several muscles may be activated at the same time, thereby counteracting the performance of one set of muscles with that of another, and thus causing generalised tension or 'freezing' – the so-called 'wooden stance' or 'tonic immobility'.

Many instances of this occurring in horses have been described in *Equine Behaviour*. Diana Lister was the first to mention it in 1986:

I have had two experiences of this in a long riding career, the first was when, as a child, I was returning home at dusk on a winter evening. The pony was a lively mare, and we had enjoyed a pleasant ride and were heading home where she would expect to have her tea. In the middle of a cross-roads in a quiet spot, she 'froze', and would not budge. With the darkness gathering, this was worrying and, as I recall, we spent possibly 15 or 20 minutes on the same spot. Despite my efforts she stood completely still with no sign of temper or concern, and eventually for no apparent

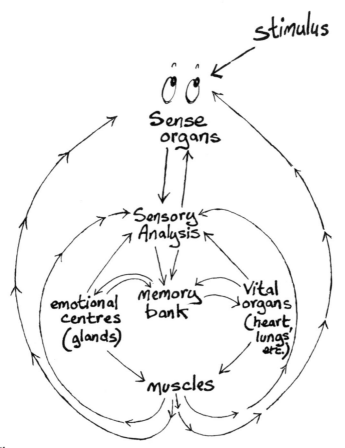

The nervous system has its headquarters in the brain

reason, she suddenly set off for home as though nothing had happened. The pony was only kept by us for a few weeks, but I rode her regularly and this was the only occasion when this problem arose.

The second occasion occurred with a large hunter mare recently purchased on trial by a friend. I was invited to take her for a short hack to try her out, but half a mile up the road she became 'wooden', and we stayed put for nearly 30 minutes while I tried everything I could think of to get her to move or show some response to my efforts. On this occasion I even dismounted and tried to lead her forward or drive her from behind. At no time was she ever upset or temperamental and, indeed, she appeared to be in a trance. After half an hour she suddenly 'came to' and consented to turn around and walk home perfectly normally.[1]

Gillian Cooper, the EBSC secretary at the time, commented:

I often had exactly the same experience with my Anglo-Arab gelding. I was in the habit of taking long hacks with him, and would often, at a suitable place, dismount and let him graze for a break. On one particular hack, there was a rarely used bridleway punctuated by gates ... where I used to take the opportunity of dismounting and untacking him and letting him graze free. On one particular day as I was about to start tacking him up I noticed the horse standing stock still, ears pricked, tail up, eyes dreaming into the distance. I could not get his head down to get the bridle on although I had thrown the reins over his head and was yanking them down hard behind the poll.[2]

A similar condition was described by many subsequent contributors to *Equine Behaviour*; for one person, sitting on top of such a horse was 'like being on a barely suppressed explosion'.[3] This is the type of behaviour that fear very often brings about when an animal realises it cannot escape and, as Dr Bryan Jones put it,

it is thought to represent the terminal reaction in a chain of anti-predator responses. Thus, if flight fails to prevent capture, the adoption of tonic immobility might reduce stimulation for further attack and cause the predator to lose interest in the prey.[4]

In the aforementioned cases, there did not seem to be anything present to evoke fear, so were the horses practising an anti-predator device, or were they rather, as several people suggested, focusing their attention on something going on in the far distance, out of sight or hearing of their riders – even, as one suggested, 'communicating by telepathy with a creature thousands of miles away'?

There are a number of causes of general muscular tension

such as the 'wooden stance', but fear is probably a common one. The presence of nervousness in riders also manifests itself through tension and stiffness, but its effect on the human body seems to vary with size and age. According to Sabrina Benson, a specialist in this area, small children tend to stiffen in the upper parts of their bodies more than in the lower, hanging on by the reins and clutching at these for support. Older and larger riders, on the other hand, tend to show their tension more by gripping the horses' sides with their legs, but leaving their hands and arms relatively loose.[5]

Moreover, there tend to be differences between the human age groups even in their approach to horses. Small children tend to be more afraid of horses and ponies when they are on the ground by their feet than when higher up on their backs, while in adults the opposite is the case. An adult is often quite happy to approach a horse in the stable or the field but becomes tense and apprehensive when mounted and being physically carried along by it.

However, 'freezing' is not the only way in which fear may affect the body. General shivering (trembling or quaking), heavy breathing through distended nostrils, breaking into a cold sweat, tightening the lips and contracting the skin so that the hair stands on end happen in the equine as well as the human body. In addition, horses can demonstrate their emotions in ways that people cannot, by means of the angle at which they hold their ears and tails. These have been very clearly illustrated in George Waring's *Horse Behaviour* (1983). They are also listed in Susan McBane's *Behaviour Problems In Horses* (1987).

Although people cannot demonstrate their emotions with tails and ears, they do, nevertheless, give themselves away by other aspects of 'body language'. Waving the hands and arms are a common way of 'letting off steam'. Tension in the facial muscles and a high-pitched tone of voice, demonstrating fear, are certainly recognised by horses, as are the scarcely perceptible (to human eyes) signs of pleasure in accomplishment.

Sensation	Position of						Muscle tension	Breathing	Voice
	Ears	Head	Eyes	Jaw and mouth	Tail	Legs			
Pain	Back	Flat	Shut	Stiff	Flat	Stiff	Tight	Heavy	Silent
Fear	Back	Up	Wide open directed to cause	Stiff	Flat	Stiff	Tight	Gasping	Squeal
Anxiety	Sideways	Up	Wide open directed to cause	Stiff	Raised slightly	Stiff	Tight	Gasping	Silent
Apprehension	Sideways	Up	Wide open directed to cause	Stiff	Raised slightly	Braced	Tight	Blowing through nostrils	Silent
Anger	Flat back	Pointed out	Looking back	Showing teeth	Whisking	Braced	Moderate	Fast	May squeal
Anticipation	Forwards	Up	Directed to cause	Stiff	High	Moving	Moderate	Moderate	Nicker
Peace	Sideways	Loose	Half closed	Relaxed	Loose	Still	Slack	Slow	Silent
Happiness	Sideways	Up	Half closed	Relaxed	Loose	May move loosely	Moderate	Moderate	Nicker
Enjoyment	Sideways	Loose	Half closed	Relaxed	Raised slightly	May move loosely	Moderate	Slightly faster	Silent
Excitement	Forwards	Up	Directed to cause	Tight	High	Moving	Stiff	Blowing	Silent
Exhaustion	Sideways	Down	Closed	Relaxed	Loose	Flagging	Loose	Heavy	Silent
Submission	Side to back	Pointed out	Half closed	Lips snapping	Flat	Braced	Moderate	Normal	Silent

Table 1. Signs of emotion

Nervousness, however, need not be as disabling as this, nor should it be confused with fear (which is usually caused by recalling a former unpleasant or painful experience) or panic. The word 'nervousness' is used here to denote only a generalised tension and discomfort accompanied by full awareness of the outside world, whereas in both fear and panic the mind tends to be fully occupied by expectations of pain or discomfort and its contact with reality is dimmed.

The Endorphins

As already mentioned, muscular tensions can be reduced by the secretion into the bloodstream of chemicals that deactivate the nerves, and some of the most important of these chemicals are the endorphins, whose circulation is controlled not through the brain, but by pressure at various points on the body: the acupressure or the acupuncture points. These points have been known to the Chinese for centuries but have only been 'scientifically' proven (and therefore generally accepted) in Europe in the last decades, thanks mainly to studies conducted in the Netherlands.

The most important of these points are:
1. The upper lip
2. The base of the neck (and along the collar)
3. The base of the spine
4. The tips of the ears

This is why people are often seen fingering their upper lips or pulling at their ear-lobes when worried about what to say or do next. It is also thought to be why curling up a horse's top lip and confining it in a twitch has such a calming effect on the nerves.

It is also probably why when two horses meet and wish to show their good intentions, they will walk up side-to-side, face each other's tail, and nibble each other's withers or croup. A rider can help to reassure a nervous horse (or show approval of its achievement) by patting its neck and 'nibbling' its withers using his or her fingers.

It is clear that a nervous individual who is always anticipating trouble must be ready to flee or freeze at any time, and that this will cause the body to use up energy at a considerable rate. Perpetually nervous horses can often be recognised by their poor physical condition. They may be poor doers who never put on flesh, or they may simply not eat when in a state of nervous anticipation or excitement.

In contrast to fear, the anticipation of something pleasant happening after an action (excitement) will activate only those muscles that are needed to perform the job and so reach the pleasant result as quickly as possible. Excitement may alternate very quickly with fear however – and vice versa – as the

This is why people are often seen fingering their upper lips

expectations swing one way or another. How a rider can help a horse to supplant fear by excitement, and so accomplish feats of strength and endurance it might otherwise never be able to achieve, is a crucial part of horsemanship, and one that will be discussed later (see Chapter IX).

The teaching of riding has come a long way since the days when horses were the only means of transport and children were thrown onto their backs as soon as they could walk and merely told to 'sit up straight' (or in the case of jumping, to 'throw your heart over it and the horse will follow'). In those days nervousness was something a rider was never allowed to admit to for fear of attracting ridicule.

As automobiles began taking over from carriages and traps and riding evolved from a necessity into a hobby, the recognition that riding is a skill that has to be learned instead of being an instinctive talent gave rise to the formation of riding schools, pony clubs and, above all, the analysis of the techniques and skills involved. This new outlook also allowed for recognition of the sensations and emotions aroused by riding, and guidelines were laid down that were based on all that we know about the mental as well as the physical processes of the human body. Many books have been written stating the dos and don'ts of how to be a good rider, but as yet none of these have really stressed the importance of nervousness and how it can be prevented or managed so as not to render disagreeable what should be enjoyable.

PART II

The Causes of Nervousness

CHAPTER II

Inheritance

Most fears are derived from associations made between a sensory stimulus and the unpleasant events that accompanied it at some point in an individual's lifetime, while some fears or reactions may have nothing to do with an actual memory, but are inherited from the parents themselves or an ancestral source.

As already mentioned, the instigation of fear begins in the sense organs (the eyes, ears, nose, mouth, skin) from where the message travels to its corresponding area in the brain. The events that accompanied these sensations during the individual's past are stored in another area of the brain – the memory bank. Outgoing messages from the bank are triggered by an incoming stimulus that alerts all the relevant areas of the body to take appropriate action.

However, the structure of the brain – as of the rest of the body – begins before the sense-organs have taken shape at all.

It starts in the genes, half of which come from the father and half from the mother, which determine not only what species of creature the fertilised egg will develop into, but also what sex it will be, what colour its hair will be, and many of the other physical and mental attributes it will possess. It is now accepted that a great many of the reactions to stimuli that arouse fear or happiness in later life, and produce either approach or avoidance reactions, are already in-bred in the new-born infant or foal.

Sex

One of the first and most basic things determined by the newly
fertilised ovum is the sex of the individual. This will play an
important part in determining not only how it will behave
towards other members of its own species, but how it will
behave in many other situations throughout its life.

In *The Horse's Mind* (1984) Lucy Rees has described many
of these differences in horses, and has stressed the not incon-
siderable effect people have on the normal behaviour of male
horses by castrating (gelding) them at an early age to make
them more tractable and amenable to the needs of their owners
instead of answering to the prompting of nature. However, not
all horses react to stressful situations in the same way, and the
differences noted by Lucy Rees in a variety of situations
seemed to be more closely related to the basic personality traits
common to the breed in general (i.e. Arab or New Forest) than
to the sex of the individual.

In humans, however, sex does seem to play quite a considerable part in initial responses both to horses and riding (see
Chapter VII).

Horses in their natural environment are among those species
preyed on by many other animals, and like all prey species they
are born with an instinctive fear of anything that moves or
looks like the type of animal that would hunt them in the wild.
These would have tended to be large animals such as the big
cats (lions, tigers, cheetahs, etc.) crouching on the ground in
long grass or scrub, and ready to pounce on them at close
range; or large reptiles, such as crocodiles, that skulk in shallow water and snap at them when they go to drink. Hence, a
horse is born with an innate tendency to look carefully at the
ground in any strange place, and to shy away from partly
hidden objects it sees there. It will also avoid stepping into
puddles – or over shiny plastic bags that simulate them! There
have been suggestions that the almost universal fear of pigs
seen in modern horses may be a hang-over of some resem-

The almost universal fear of pigs seen in modern horses

blance between today's pigs and the ancestral predators of the equids.

The survival of the species as a whole depended originally on living in herds, so that if one member of the herd was caught, other members of the family might survive and breed replacements. For this reason, horses abhor solitude. Moreover, as their ancestors survived by outrunning their predators, confinement (in a stable, for instance) is another natural fear that modern horse management has to overcome.

However, it is not only stables that restrict a horse's movement and prevent it from running away from possible predators. Anything attached to its head (like a bridle or head-collar) that prevents it from 'taking off' – its most natural and instinctive method of escape – is likely to cause anxiety in the early stages of a horse's life. Most breeders of domestic horses or ponies will be only too familiar with this problem; it is not uncommon for a foal, that may have been only too happy to eat out of its owner's hand or follow him or her into and out of stables since birth, to put up quite a struggle when it first feels a strap or rope over its nose and finds that it can no longer walk away when it wants to.

For infantile humans lack of physical support of the head in the first days of life is not only fear-provoking but can be dangerous. When a small child is first put on the back of a pony, the sense of insecurity that results (until it has learned to balance itself) can last a lifetime. I still remember the terror I felt when, still scarcely able to walk unaided, I was lifted onto the back of a Shetland pony. Today, children are not encouraged to ride until they are in full control of their own bodies at around the age of seven, and until they have become accustomed to handling a pony in its field or stable, have led it around, and touched its back and legs. It cannot be emphasised too strongly that while nervousness of the strange and unknown are only sensible and healthy, the sensation of pain or fear associated with a first-time experience should be avoided if at all possible, as it can so easily result in permanent dislike of that object or activity.

Another essential for equine happiness is freedom and comfort of the feet and legs – those parts of the horse's body that are relied on to save it from death in a race against predators. The first attempts by humans to touch these vital regions are regarded by horses with great suspicion, while at the same time these are the areas that most often *need* human attention. 'No foot, no horse' is a well-worn old adage, and none is truer. The way this attention is given, from a horse's very earliest hours until its death, needs careful consideration if trouble is to be avoided.

Even having a foot held up off the ground is frightening for a young horse, and habituation to this necessity cannot be started too young. Furthermore, for a hind shoe to be fixed, the horse has to be prepared to stand with one hindleg held out behind it in an unnatural position, and to have its hoof pierced with nails and then hammered. Perhaps the hardest thing of all for horses, however, is the flow of smoke around their heads when a hot shoe burns their foot as it is being checked for shape. One farrier told me that he always tries to get a young horse to stand up close to an older one that he is dealing with, so that it can see the process being carried out before its own turn comes.

Sights

The *direction* from which an unknown object approaches can also be threatening. In the case of people, who probably originated from tree-living anthropoids, attacks from above (e.g. from angry birds whose fruit they were eating) were probably more common than attacks from the ground; hence the inborn tendency in humans, even today, is to duck their heads when anything swoops down towards them from above, like a low-flying aircraft, which horses in general tend to ignore completely. Terror of even small flying creatures like bats or moths (which are probably more likely to *be* hurt by people than vice versa) as well as of creepy-crawlies like worms and spiders, are also common causes of panic among humans.

The horse's natural enemies were creatures that often attacked from behind by jumping on its back or biting its hindlegs, so it is only natural that horses should have an inborn fear of having a rider sitting on their backs and of having traffic coming up behind them on roads, while at the same time being prevented from running forwards by the bit in their mouths. Very great care is needed when introducing horses to these necessities of riding.

Whether the actual side of the body from which a strange object approaches makes a difference has long been debated. Because the majority of humans are right-handed, they tend to be more aware of things on that side of their body than the other, but this does not seem to be the case with horses, although 'onesidedness' is often quite a problem when they

Creepy-crawlies like worms and spiders are also common causes of panic

start working. However, this is probably because humans, being right-handed, tend to approach and handle horses more often from the horse's left (the near) side than the right (the off side). The asymmetry of the internal organs is another factor that has been put forward to account for onesidedness. The left ventricle of the horse's heart, like that of the human, is larger than the right, and, as Professor Vogel has emphasised, the nerve supplying the left side of the horse's larynx follows a longer route than that on the right and hence is more likely to become strained or paralysed.[1]

In general, however, horses show no preference for using

one foreleg rather than the other for such acts as pawing the ground, leading over a jump, or leading off from halt. Bernard Grzimek published a study[2] on this subject in 1969 and Frank Ödberg confirmed his findings later that year.[3] Sometimes injury or accident leads to one leg being used more freely than another, but this tendency is confined to individual animals.

I myself had a hunch that the right-sided stiffness, seen in so many adult horses when first ridden, might have its origin in suckling. In order to suckle, a foal has to bend its head and neck to one side, and it seemed logical to suspect that if such flexion was strongly established in the young animal, it might be reverted to in later life, when the mouth and gums were stimulated by the bit. In the spring of 1971, therefore, I carried out a survey on three different types of horse – Thoroughbred, hunter and New Forest pony – and watched 73 different foals take a total of 211 drinks, noting the side of the dam from which they did so.

Contrary to my hypothesis, the foals of all three breeds and at all places tended to drink slightly more often from the right (off side) than from the left (near side), thereby bending their necks towards the right, but the differences were too small to be significant. Moreover, only five of the seventeen foals that I was able to watch drinking on more than one occasion, showed any consistent preference for side.

Returning to the question of whether the *direction* from which a strange object first appears has an effect on the emotional reactions it evokes in horses, this was investigated by members of the EBSC, who undertook a project to study the matter during 1987–8, by watching their own horses in their own home settings.

Each member took a strange object (e.g. a white plastic bag), placed it in various settings, and noted their horses' reactions to it, particularly signs of nervousness, which might be seen in the size of the pupils of the eyes, any movements of the ears or nostrils, muscular stiffness, or movements towards or away from the object:

1. When it was placed in a familiar and an unfamiliar setting
2. When it was stationary above and below the horse's head
3. When it was moving towards and away from the horse
4. When it was first seen in front and behind by the horse

Seven members of the EBSC and their families took part in the investigation, and their horses – fifteen in all – covered most breeds and ages. From the variety of results and responses that were reported it was obvious that there was no clear-cut answer to the question, but that only more questions were raised by the complexity of the reports received. From the reactions of my own horses in the above-mentioned situations, I concluded that neither the position nor the activity of a strange object really had a great effect on a horse's emotional responses to it. Of far greater importance were:

1. The horse's own basic temperament
2. Its past experiences in novel situations
3. Its mood at the moment of perception

A possible explanation for all this was suggested by Dr T. R. Roberts:

There is still a great deal of mystery about what goes on during an act of recognition. Indeed, the elucidation of this mystery may turn out to be the most difficult of all the current problems in neurophysiological enquiry. It is not always appreciated how important a part the act of recognition plays in any stimulus-response situation. Even a coin-operated slot machine has to have a mechanism for 'recognising' that a coin has been inserted and that certain dimensions of that coin fall between prescribed limits. The mechanism may, for example, incorporate a device for rejecting discs with holes in them (such as washers) if it is intended to be operated only by coins of the realm.

Context is important. We tend to think of our world as made up of discrete objects, each of which is distinguished as separate from the background. We persist in this type of interpretation even when looking at pictures in which the patches of colour contributing to our image of an object are, in themselves, indistinguishable from similar patches of colour 'representing' the background in the same picture. There is no reason to suppose that animals behave similarly to ourselves in separating 'figure' from 'ground'. Thus what we may think of as a familiar object may, to a horse, constitute an alarm signal when it is presented in surroundings where it does not otherwise commonly appear. Any unfamiliar detail in a horse's environment might indicate the approach of a predator – just the sort of warning sign that a potential prey must be continually on the lookout for.

This brings out an important difference between humans and horses in the way they learn new things. The differences may reflect a fundamental difference between predator and prey species. A predator is not easily discouraged by failure. The behaviour is characterised by the saying 'if at first you don't succeed, try, try, and try again'. For the prey, on the other hand, it is important for his survival that he should avoid situations in which he has previously had occasion to be alarmed. The relevant saying here is 'once bitten, twice shy'. Man, being partly a carnivore, counts as a predator, while the horse, which is exclusively herbivorous, belongs to a prey species.[4]

Other differences between horses and men will be dealt with in later chapters, but here let it be noted that although we may not know exactly what goes on in recognition, horses do seem to be very aware of, and react quite strongly to, all alterations in a familiar place. Mary Good describes this most vividly. Her five-year-old Arab mare had been on holiday in Derbyshire where she had been ridden over the hills and moors but not on the roads . . .

so before the January snows started we brought her back to Ewloe (where I live). The first time out on the road, she 'looked' at a pile of bricks outside a newly-built house but walked quite happily past. She stopped and had to be coerced round two fencing poles with a roll of sheep wire loosely wound round them and lying in the hedge. The second day the pile of bricks had changed shape. She paused but walked on quietly. At the poles and wire we still had to talk her past but in much less time she went on, although giving them a rather wide berth.

The third day, she stopped at the pile of bricks – it had changed into half a gatepost and stood about three feet high. That worried her more than before but nevertheless, she walked past, but kept a good eye on it in case it changed shape again. The post and wire bothered her not at all. She snorted briefly to let it be known she had seen them, but otherwise she just walked past without hesitation. That then caused no further problems. But the following day, the gatepost had been completed *and* a plastic cover put over it. That created a great quandary. She whipped round. I was riding her at the time, so kept her turning and we faced it again. She was more reluctant to go past it than past the posts and wire which she had originally baulked at to a much greater degree.

The next few days, the gatepost remained unchanged and she accepted that and walked past. *But* the last time we went past, the plastic cover had been removed and again the changed shape unsettled her. I am inclined to think that the continually altering outline will make her suspicious of that particular house for quite a while yet![5]

Fire

Although it can be fatally damaging, fire can also be very exciting and comforting to all animals. At one time it was believed that humans alone among animals had learned to overcome an inate fear of fire and had been able to make use of it to arm themselves against possible enemies and drive cave-dwelling animals from their cosy lairs. It is true that as yet no other species has developed the skill of making fire, but it has recently been discovered that many species of birds are adept at gathering firebrands and carrying them to convenient roosting posts where they will preen themselves before the smoking embers – an activity called 'anting'.[6]

Nor is it only birds that are attracted by the warmth and glow of flames. Those of us who keep cats and dogs in our houses and who still maintain an open hearth will know that far from shunning the heat, our pets often have to be forcibly restrained from hogging the whole fireside area. The presence of a bonfire in an enclosure inhabited by cattle or horses acts as a magnet to these animals too. I was able to demonstrate this by marking off a portion of a 5 ha (12 acre) field inhabited by five horses and 30 head of cattle, and keeping a watch for three consecutive days to count the number of animals that were within the area at every hour between 8.00 a.m. and 8.00 p.m.

At 11.00 a.m. on the second day, a heap of dried straw was taken into the centre of the marked area and set alight, the fire lasting until about 4.00 p.m. that afternoon when a heavy storm extinguished it. The results of the counts are shown in Table 2.

It will be seen that the area was hardly occupied at all on the first and third days, but that for three to four hours immedi-

A bonfire in an enclosure inhabited by cattle or horses acts as a magnet to these animals

Time of day (Hours)	9	10	11	12	13	14	15	16	17	18	19	20
Before		3				2		2	2			
During				*4	14	19	19	14	3			
After		2										

* Bonfire laid and lit

Table 2. Showing the number of animals out of 35 standing in the marked area of the field on three successive days, before, during and after the bonfire was lit

ately following the lighting of the fire, both cattle and horses gathered within it.

Movement

Ever since the wheel was invented, it has posed a problem in our relationship with horses. As already mentioned, the horse's chief predators in the wild were creatures that stalked it from behind and pounced on its back; so when a horse is attached to a rickety vehicle that clatters along behind it on large, unsightly wheels, it must awaken all its deepest and most basic urges for self-protection.

Replacement of the animal-drawn vehicle by the motorised version has only changed the problem, not removed it; for nowadays a horse is more often than not transported itself in this leviathan. Entering the box or trailer must seem literally like walking into the jaws of death; and as the doors clang shut and the external world vanishes from view, the feeling must be something like that of being swallowed alive. It is not surprising that horses need very careful introduction to the phenomenon, and equally careful management once they are in. Dr Sharon Cregier has made a special study[7] of this subject, and largely as a result of her work it is now accepted that the old-fashioned, forward-facing trailer – in which, as the vehicle brakes, all the animal's weight is thrown forward onto its front

legs instead of backwards onto its much stronger hindquarters
– should be avoided.

The difficulties facing horses in modern mechanised transport – on the sea and in the air as well as on the roads – and how
these can be minimised, have been described by Chris Larter
and Tony Jacklin in *Transporting Your Horse or Pony* (1987).
However, it is not just being physically connected to, or
transported by, a wheeled vehicle that frightens horses; meet-
ing one on the road, or being passed by one coming up from
behind is very scaring at the first encounter.

In the early days of the EBSC, Marion Boyle collected and
analysed a great deal of information on the subject, supplied to
her by members of the circle. This revealed some unique
experiences, including one that happened to her:

> I thought we were going to have three traffic-shy horses, after an
> accident recently on the road beside their field. One car somer-
> saulted over the hedge to land a few feet away from them after an
> accident. However, we took the horses out to the road the next
> day. The bossy two-year-old looked rather alert and aggressive,
> and struck out with a front foot at a bus which passed very close (he
> was in the farm gateway). The others ignored everything.[8]

Her final conclusions were that the commonest fear-producing
stimuli on the roads seemed to be:

1. Large moving objects. Many horses that ignore passing cars
   shy at lorries and buses
2. Vehicles coming very close: a quiet country lane may not
   be so pleasant to hack along if you meet a tractor in the
   confined space
3. The sound and feeling of water sprayed up from puddles by
   passing traffic
4. Vehicles partly hidden, e.g. by the rider's leg
5. Reflections in windows on a sunny day: this may cause a
   horse to shy at a parked vehicle that it would normally
   ignore

6. Certain sounds, e.g. hissing air brakes, loud roars, two-stroke engines, angry and threatening voices
7. A succession of vehicles passing one after another or one stationary or slow-moving one. Many horses will face up to the momentary presence of something threatening, as long as it goes away quickly rather than maintaining a continuing threat

Horses are not the only animals that can be upset by movement over which they have no control. For first-time riders, the sensation of being moved along by something underneath them can also be very unnerving and some novices take quite some time to relax.

Sounds

Any scraping, grating or rasping sound evokes unpleasant sensations in most animals, including people, and an electrical clipping machine working around the head and ears is particularly frightening to horses. It probably arouses the same sort of sensation that a dentist's drill does in a human, setting the teeth on edge and the nerves jangling. Ways in which this fear can be prevented or overcome will be discussed later (see Chapter IV).

Sudden loud bangs will make all creatures jump, and sheer volume of noise alone may cause permanent damage to the ear drums if kept up for any length of time. Loud sounds repeated at constant intervals, however, can be acclimatised to by horses much more easily than by humans, which is probably one reason why horses are less upset than people by the proximity of busy airports.

Many sounds can have a very soothing effect. Music, for example, can be both calming and exhilarating, as was reported by Michael Osborn of the Irish National Stud.[9] The Kildare Yard is newly built with three types of stabling – a conventional stable yard for 22 horses, a barn-type building for 22 horses, and a standing stall (open plan) building for 22 horses.

Sudden loud bangs will make all creatures jump

All three buildings are wired for sound, using an amplifier and speakers. During the two years prior to 1980, the staff used the system to try out different musical sounds, and found a noticeable difference in the horses' reactions. Soft, orchestral music had a soporific effect, while loud, heavy-beat rock music was agitating. Many other studs (and livery yards) also play taped music to their charges, and have found that it can be a great help in calming newcomers – if the right sort of tune is selected!

The equine appreciation of rhythm has recently been shown up strongly in the increasingly popular 'dressage to music' exhibitions and competitions. Indeed, horses trained in the technique have demonstrated that they are just as capable of keeping time to the music on the end of a lunge-line as they are under saddle.

The ability of horses (as of dogs and many other species) to recognise the approach of their owners not only by their voices but also by the sound of their cars, has often been described, and their sensitivity in this respect is probably far greater than ours.

Fear of the Unknown

Not knowing what to expect in the future is a frightening situation for all animals. Times of crisis brought on by irregularities of weather (floods, storms, droughts) or by territorial battles leading to food shortages are extremely perturbing to people as well as to horses but once a routine is established (even if it is not a particularly comfortable one) relaxation can set in. The routine need not be identical for all members of a herd for it to be satisfying; it has recently come to light that horses are extremely adaptable to individual routines. Those kept in do-it-yourself livery yards, and fed by their attendants at different times, will quickly come to expect their rations only on the appearance of their regular feeders, and will not get upset at seeing other horses around them being fed by their own attendants.

It is also essential for the peace of mind of a group of animals – and here I include people as well as horses – to establish a *social hierarchy* within the group, so that each individual knows who to look to for leadership or whose orders must be obeyed. In most groups, age and past experience are the main characteristics of the group leader, but physical or mental prowess can well enable a younger member of the group to supplant an established boss, while skirmishes among the also-rans are a common feature of all societies.

The two situations mentioned above – an uncertain future and a muddled social hierarchy – interact to a large extent. Thus, a totally new situation can be less frightening if a trusted leader is present as a guide, and here the 'leader' can be just as effective if it belongs to a different species altogether. The fear that overcomes a young horse that is taken to a busy showground or out hunting for the first time can be appeased (or turned into excitement) by a trusted and experienced rider, and the same goes for an inexperienced rider who is mounted on a horse or pony that knows how it is expected to behave in these novel circumstances.

Entering unknown territory can also be very scaring. To a horse, being asked to jump over an obstacle that blocks its vision of the landing side must be like asking a human to run into a dark cave. I have known horses schooled to perfection over 1.5 m (5 ft) fences they can see through (like showjumping poles) who would still balk at a solid wall 90 cm (3 ft) high until they had developed confidence in their riders' judgement.

Phobias

In addition to the inborn fears that affect all members of a species, some genetic lines within that species develop their own idiosyncratic 'phobias', which may be evident from birth or may only become apparent at a certain stage of maturity. In humans, members of the male sex commonly have an acute fear of horses; and the psychoanalyst Sigmund Freud dealt with one such case at a fairly early stage in his career.

Although Freud's interpretation of the causes of the horse-phobia in this case may not have been completely correct, there is no doubt that many men – and women – do have phobias stemming from early childhood, and that a fear of horses, although a comparatively common one, is not the only cause of phobias. Water, heights, fire, open spaces and certain insects are other common causes; and it is characteristic of such fears that they tend to run in families.

Horse 'families', i.e. horses that are closely related, are recognised to have curious idiosyncracies. I have had personal experience of this with one line of horses that had a phobia about entering stables. The family was descended from a chestnut mare who came to be covered by a stallion I owned at that time.

The result of this union – a bay filly whom I named Gem – was put up for sale by her breeder as a three-year-old because as a yearling she had escaped from her stable, climbed into a field containing her owner's colts and got herself in foal. From the first day of Gem's arrival at my yard, she showed a great reluctance to enter stables. She could be led to the doorway without difficulty but, once there, would throw her nose in the air as high as possible and rush backwards. I immediately assumed she must have had a fright at some time in her life, causing her to hit her head on a low roof. However, even after weeks of daily pushing, cajoling, and eventually forcing her inside (where she was always rewarded with a welcome feed), she was still hesitant at the doorway, and even six years later would 'play up' if a strange horse or person came into the yard. In other respects, however, she was unflappable.

Gem's three offspring to date – all chestnuts – have been extremely headshy from birth and, just like Gem, will occasionally stick their noses in the air and rush off in reverse when asked to enter a stable. The third one, when a foal, was the most difficult youngster to put a head-collar on that I have ever met. Every time, he had to be cornered up against his mother in a stable before he could be touched, and it would then take up to 30 minutes of soothing, coaxing and stroking before his jaw would relax and he would begin to look around. Day after day, for the first six months of his life, the battle continued, and then, two days after he had been weaned, it stopped. The problem was inclined to return again, however, if anything unexpected happened, like a stranger entering the stable yard.

The fear of being stabled is comparatively common – as is apparent from the number of reports on the subject received from members of the EBSC – and probably stems from the 'herd' instinct; but stables are not the only thing to cause acute, unreasonable and apparently inherited fear. Mrs Pegg from Norfolk wrote to describe her five-year-old skewbald mare, Mystery:

Mystery's dam was bought by my uncle about ten years ago and was about 8 years old at the time. Ever since we have had her she has had an intense dislike of dogs, almost bordering on hatred . . . if any dogs should go into the field or go anywhere near her, she will really go for them, ears flat back and ready to attack with teeth and hooves.

My uncle has a farm, and as most members of the family have an interest in horses, there are quite a few horses kept there. Mystery was bred on the farm and was brought up with dogs around as a matter of course. She has always been kept with other horses and ponies who take no notice of dogs. She has, however, followed in her dam's footsteps and seems to have an aversion to dogs. She is not as bad as her mother and will not go out of her way to attack them, but she is always ready to kick out with either front or back feet should one stray too near her hooves. She has not had any bad experience with dogs so it seems just to have been passed on from her dam. The strange thing is, there are also free-range chickens kept on the farm, and those can wander around in complete safety. They can peck around right between Mystery's hooves and she takes no notice of them at all.[10]

In the cases of Gem and Mystery, although the inherited fears were accompanied by particular coat-colours (chestnut in the first, skewbald in the second), it is not to be assumed that all horses with a particular coat-colour inherit the same fears. It is true that 'temperamental' traits may be associated with pigmentation of the hair in both horses and people (chestnut horses, like red-headed people, tend to have short fuses), but this is very different from the terror, characteristic of a real phobia, that is evoked by certain specific stimuli. Although some phobias may be innate, it does not follow that they are incurable; how they can be dealt with is discussed later (see Chapter V).

As I suggested in *Horse Psychology* (1976), colour-linked temperamental differences may be associated with different distributions of sensory nerve-endings in the skin. In albinos there is no doubt that sensory deficiencies in the eyes coincide with a lack of pigmentation in the skin; so that the lack of pigmentation in greys as a whole may well be accompanied by a sparsity of sensory nerves in the skin, making them frequently docile and easy to handle. Whether this is universally the case (rather than following specific family lines) seems to be uncertain, but what *is* certain is that the depth and richness of a horse's coat are also dependent on:

1. The nutrition it is receiving
2. The amount of grooming it receives
3. In the case of mares, whether she is in season or not

CHAPTER III

Growing Up

Although the basic pattern of the nervous system is inherited and is present at birth, the way it develops – and the way the neural pathways (from sense organs via the brain to the muscles) develop during an individual's life – depends very largely on experience.

In general, the younger an animal is at the time of a new experience, the more likely it is to repeat the pattern of behaviour aroused by that experience (and hence the more deeply ingrained that response-pattern becomes). However, much depends on the emotions that are aroused by the stimuli at the same time as the behaviour takes place, or on those emotions aroused by events immediately following the behaviour. In common terms, 'pleasure strengthens, displeasure weakens' the tendency for repetition, but repetition itself is a very important strengthener of bonds. It establishes 'habits' – behaviour-patterns that tend to be performed spontaneously, i.e. without any voluntary effort on the part of the performer – and the more *often* a habit is performed, the harder it becomes to change or modify.

Play

During early life, many of the horse's bonds to the herd are established through play. The serious study of play is comparatively recent in the history of science – although the importance of its role in human education has long been recognised. Since 1970, the nature and importance of play in animals has also been the subject of many publications. Several EBSC members have observed and described play behaviour in their own horses. In June 1988, Professor Andrew Fraser reported:

The process in the horse starts at birth when those parts of the foal's neuro-muscular system concerned with fighting and fleeing begin to develop. Fight and flight are essential for the survival of herd-living animals such as horses; but as the new-born foal is normally protected by its dam, the neuro-muscular requirements for those activities only develop through play-fights which, when indulged in satisfactorily, are accompanied by an emotional excitement and sense of fulfilment. When play is denied, as in chronic confinement, an outburst of play activity is usually seen in these animals on being released.

Although the movements of play are like those seen in serious situations, the emotional accompaniments (as evidenced by the foal's vocal expressions) are very different. Instead of the anger of a fight or the fear of flight, the squeals made in play suggest enjoyment. The movements required in play are basically innate and patterned at birth, but their perfection is only acquired with practice.

Play has mixed goals and roles. As the foal first leaves its mother's womb, its body has to face up to new situations. At birth, each system of the body has a limited blood supply, and the future supply to the system depends on the extent to which it is activated. This activation is a vital function of play. If energy has to be conserved to safeguard the blood supply to vital organs (as may occur in cold and wet weather, or if nutritious food is in short supply) play will not take place. However, after prolonged confinement or inactivity, the release of the foal will result in an outburst of excitement suggesting a release from tension and discomfort.

Among a group of foals, social play usually increases, and solitary play decreases with age, so that by the time they are 2 months old, solitary play is reduced to almost zero. In lone foals, however, solitary play – or play with other animal species and even with inanimate objects – may continue for longer.

Mutual grooming bouts and oral 'snapping' often initiate play, but the commonest form of play between foals involves nipping of

Among a group of foals, social play usually increases with age

the head and mane, gripping the crest, rearing up towards one another, chasing, mounting and side-to-side fighting. There are sex differences in play, colts mounting more frequently than fillies, and in general being more vigorous. Most play involves nipping or biting; but running along alone or in groups with sudden stops and starts, chasing, tossing the head, and kicking up the hind legs are also typical.

Usually foals prefer to play with others of the same age as themselves, and after the first four weeks of life (during which they will only play close to their mothers and alone) indulging in solo gambols, will wander off in search of play-mates; and as social play develops it involves chasing and reverse-chasing, butting, neck-wrestling, and mutual rearing. This may merge into low intensity fighting to determine position or rank in animals just entering a sub-adult society. As juveniles, this locomotor and manipulative activity is often repeated with slight variations – such as jumps vertically away from the mother and back to her – and the manipulation of objects after they have been explored and inspected.[1]

Play does not necessarily stop after youth in horses any more than in people, as has often been noted by members of the EBSC. In 1979, Christine Belton described how her horse, before it had been gelded, used to pick up sticks or pieces of cardboard and 'gallop round the field waving them up and down'.[2]

In the same issue of *Equine Behaviour*, Janet MacDonald wrote about Jasper, owned by her for over five years. Jasper, too, would pick up a stick and, when turned out with other horses, would lead them on a gallop round the field, usually if he knew he had an audience. 'After Jasper had been in the field a couple of months, I found that the stick game had been extended into a full-scale game of "I've got the stick; you can't catch me". I later acquired a New Forest pony who also joined in the game.'[3]

In 1981, Anne Eley described (and sketched) a similar game played by her horses – three geldings and a mare.[4]

The tendency for colts and geldings to mouth and bite objects in play more often than mares is not confined to the British Isles. In 1982 Veronica Snowden worked with horses in Spain for six months. She wrote:

These horses work from March to November and then have three months' rest, during the winter. The farm where they are kept has no grazing. It is rare for horses to be kept out or even turned out unless tethered, but there is a small dust corral where they are let loose for half the day since they get no other exercise. I was told by my employer that last winter, on several occasions, he saw the

geldings playing a similar 'stick game'. One horse, who is particularly playful – the type who can undo literally *any* knot and escape
from anywhere – would pick up a stick, there being many in the
corral, holding it in his mouth, shaking it, and rearing up.

Other horses would join in, trying to take the stick from him,
involving much rearing, chasing and shaking of the stick. They
would play other games such as shadow boxing, generally amusing
themselves since there was no grazing to keep them occupied, and
no space for a good gallop to use up their energy. The stick game, if
I recall correctly, was only played by the geldings. The mares, who
were turned out separately, would shadow box, more so than the
geldings, but did not invent so many games. Whilst in work during
the summer, the horses were turned out for shorter spells, and I
never witnessed such games, so it appears the horses only invented
these during their more boring rest months.[5]

Games with riders are another variation that was described
in 1984 by Anne James. Harry was an eight-year-old Thoroughbred gelding that she began riding:

When I was young and innocent and believed what I read in books,
one of the commandments was 'thou shalt not punish a horse for
shying', and it did seem logical that if the horse was frightened by
an object he should be coaxed and encouraged to approach it and
assure himself that it was not dangerous. The trouble was that
Harry appeared to be frightened of everything – cigarette packets
on the verge, fertiliser bags in the hedge, fallen leaves blowing in
the autumn, large leaves showing a light underside in the spring
breezes – in fact, anything that was even mildly conspicuous.

Small things produced spectacular sideways leaps, large things
produced really fast sensational whip-rounds from any gait,
followed by a gallop away. So I was patient (often frightened, too)
and spoke kindly while trying to persuade him to go forward.
Sometimes when things were really bad I got off and tried to lead
him up to the problem. All to no avail – when I went for a ride I
never knew when I would get back. Even the last hundred yards
home could take half an hour if there was something strange in the
hedge. Local opinion labelled Harry a standard chestnut lunatic,
mad and dangerous.

But gradually, I began to wonder why I never fell off and why he
had no scars or lumps on his legs. The more I thought about it the

Harry appeared to be frightened of everything

more I realised how careful he always was to look before he leapt and to keep well clear of ditches, deep mud, barbed wire, lorries, etc. If I lost my balance and slipped sideways he always stopped and let me recover before rushing off again. Somewhat belatedly, I realised he wasn't really frightened of anything – he was playing. So I changed my tactics and found that by being really angry and using my voice and whip, he would usually pass even major things at the second or third attempt, but I was never able to do more than shorten the game; he wouldn't give it up entirely. He seemed to love an audience and was always at his worst riding out with other horses. Big, elaborate spooks at everyday objects induced near nervous breakdowns in my friends' normal serious minded horses, and the chaos he could cause during a lesson in the indoor school had to be seen to be believed, as the other horses got more and more twitchy and uptight, looking for the dangers which Harry was reacting to so dramatically.[6]

In 1987, EBSC members were asked to make notes of the games played by their horses, and describe in detail:

1. With whom the games were most often played
2. When the games were played

Joy Partridge noted that the games played by her horse (a nine-year-old gelding who had been owned by her since the age of four), when turned out with other horses, in addition to the run-and-kick games described by Andrew Fraser, included a game with her when she was bringing him in in the evenings, when he would nip the backs of her boots and try to toss her into the air. Most games were played in bright, blustery weather, and when waiting to come in in the evenings.[7]

Mrs Dunn, the owner of a nine-year-old Arab mare, Sayyida, and a fourteen-year-old Dales-cross gelding, Gareth, noted that when they were in the field together they usually grazed side by side, but occasionally one would want to move onto new pastures:

> This will start a little game which is often played between them, when the one who wishes to move on pushes the other from behind. If Sayyida is at the receiving end she will give a little squeal, but there is no stress shown whatsoever. She will then move as requested. However Gareth, when nudged from the rear by Sayyida will just amble on, and she will generally keep on nudging in the direction she wishes him to take. It is obvious to the onlooker that this is great fun for both, as they play for quite lengthy periods of time.[8]

Mrs Dunn also noticed that playing with objects was quite common in the stables, where Sayyida would use her empty feed-bin as a football or a footbath, and out in the field:

> Gareth will pick on some object in the field, it could be a plant, twig, droppings or a cat; and snort down his nostrils with his neck outstretched and his ears pricked forward like radar; and then pretend it is a monster and turn round on his hind legs and gallop flat out down the field, before turning round and trotting sedately

back to his starting position. If he feels like doing it again, he will; otherwise he will just graze quietly.[9]

The fear initially aroused by a strange object will often turn into a game played with or around it, as if to 'let off the steam' aroused by clenched muscles, and for this reason it is not always easy to tell when a horse is really frightened of passing certain objects or places, and when its fear has subsided and been turned into a game with its rider or handler.

The dividing line between fear and fun in riders is very narrow – but let it not be imagined that bad feelings always turn into good! Instances are only too common of injuries – even fatal ones – being sustained in play.

Communication

All living creatures have methods of vocal or visual communication (languages) that enable them to interact with one another, and in the majority of birds and mammals these include signals that have to be learned during youth from family or friends. Horses communicate mainly through gestures of the facial organs – snapping or mouthing with the lips; the position of the ears – but squeals and grunts are also common, as described in several books on the subject.[10]

Failure to learn these signals in infancy – either as a result of isolation or from deficiencies in the nervous system (blindness, deafness, or a deformity in the cerebral area that normally deals with them, as in autism) – can ruin the quality of an individual's whole life. In humans, such problems have been recognised for many years, but it has only fairly recently been accepted that a similar situation occurs in horses. The hand-rearing of foals whose dams had died giving birth or who had been unable to suckle them, was at one time fairly common, and the affection and dependence shown by such animals towards their pseudo-parents was taken as a compliment or an act of gratitude. Only in the last decades has it come to be realised that this can have fatal consequences for the foal itself, which, because it fails to appreciate and respond appropriately to the demands or commands of its elders when turned out in fields with them, may well be set upon, chased or kicked to death.

I had a personal experience of this many years ago. A friend and neighbour, who was a vet, used to hand-rear orphan foals for her clients. She asked me to run one of them out with my own young stock after it had been weaned and while its owners were abroad. I found myself having to spend many days (and nights!) running out to the foal's assistance when it failed to make the required 'I surrender' signal (a snapping of the mouth with the lips drawn back and the ears and eyes turned to the sides) after it had inadvertently usurped the food or the resting place preferred by the group leader. However, the worst happened after the foal had been returned to its owner; it was chased through a fence and landed up with a broken neck.

This example illustrates the importance of being able to receive and decode, as well as give, signals, and it is just as essential in the communication between people and horses as it is between two people or two horses. Thus, a rider or handler must be able to listen to and interpret what the horse is saying to him or her just as adequately as he or she tells it what to do.

Cases are known of horses being much better (and quicker) than humans at learning the 'body language' of other species. A classical instance was that of 'Clever Hans', who at one time acquired the reputation of being a mathematical genius, and who was exhibited by his owner, Herr von Osten, throughout Europe in an attempt to prove that horses were just as intelligent as humans and only required educating in the same way.

Herr von Osten set about teaching Hans mathematics, by writing simple sums on a blackboard and getting Hans to tap out the answers to them using one forefoot to denote the tens and the other to denote the single numbers. In quite a short time, Hans learned what was required of him and how to tap out the answers. At this point Herr Von Osten began touring various seats of learning, demonstrating the horse's skill. At

Clever Hans

one such demonstration, however, the learned audience suspected a hoax, and a commission was set up to investigate the matter.

The commission concluded that there was no intentional hoax, as Hans was apparently still able to solve the problems when Herr von Osten was out of sight and unaware of the problem set – so long as others within sight of Hans *did* know the problem and its correct answer. It was then noticed that

Hans seemed much more interested in watching the person posing the problem than in the problem itself, and moreover that the questioners were making slight, and quite unconscious, movements of the head and eyes every time Hans reached the correct number of taps with each foot. If the questioners and audience were hidden from Hans's view, the poor horse was all at sea.

When this was demonstrated to him, Herr Von Osten's despair was complete. He not only gave up all his claims about equine intelligence, but lost all interest in Hans as well, who is said to have been retired to his owner's estate to live out the rest of his life in forlorn solitude. However, this reaction would seem unjustified. Hans may not have been solving the mathematical problems set him, but he was solving some of far more importance to himself, namely the meaning of human body language, and how to gain his rewards.

Normal, healthy human adults are often rather reluctant to 'listen' to what animals are saying to them (preferring just to give orders rather than indulge in genuine communication); and this is probably one reason why mentally and physically handicapped people – who are accustomed to receiving commands and are usually pretty expert at reading body language – seem to get on so well with horses.

Education and Schooling

In both horses and humans, learning depends, in the early days, on forming associations between an experience and its accompaniments or after-effects, i.e. rewards or punishments. For the latter to have much significance for the horse, however, they have to follow the experience very quickly, or the two will not be associated. Horses are taught that sounds like 'whoa' and 'walk on' are signals to stop and go. Whatever the lesson, it is essential that the pupil can understand what constitutes a right or wrong response, and this is done by the teacher giving a reward or punishment in association with the response – a verbal 'Yes' or 'No' to a human and a gentle pat or a sharp slap to a horse. Uncertainty about the meaning of a signal, i.e. what response it should evoke, is one of the chief causes of nervousness in all creatures. It is therefore very important for an animal's trainer to be absolutely consistent about what behaviour is acceptable and what behaviour is not.

In order to save horses from confusion, it is important that the signals given by all riders to all horses (the aids) are the same the world over. I discovered this many years ago when I was experimenting with the use of different aids for showjumpers (see Chapter VIII). I had the idea that by giving aids to the horses solely through placing my hands in different positions on their withers, I could improve their ability to jump by leaving their heads free to enable them to balance themselves around corners or when stopping and starting. The task of teaching my aids was not difficult (circus trainers habitually teach their animals to respond to signals that the audience are not expected to recognise), but the horses' obedience to them amazed even me. However, I found myself bound (almost literally) to care for and exercise my horses myself, as no one else could communicate with them. This taught me the value of a common set of aids for use between all horses and riders.

The speed with which an individual, human or equine, learns used to be considered to depend on 'intelligence', but the whole concept of intelligence, and what it involves, has come to be rather confused in recent years. Speed of learning (i.e. the number of trials it takes to learn that '2 + 2 = 4') was at one time considered the only possible way to measure it, but then it came to be realised that some individuals took longer to learn such simple associations than other things, like finding their way out of mazes, how to solve puzzles or how to put things together. Moreover, as pointed out by Gillian Cooper,[11] horses have many different ways of solving a problem, and who is to say that one solution is more intelligent than another? This was demonstrated in a livery yard where each horse had its own way of removing the lid from a food container. One did so carefully, holding the container with a foot and lifting the lid with its teeth; whereas another simply kicked the whole container against the wall, breaking it open. Both methods were equally effective in their result for the horses, although one might seem to us to be stupider than the other.

Moreover, different animal species vary in their aptitudes for learning different types of task. Horses, for example, appear to be excessively slow at learning to find their way *around* obstacles (the detour problem). They are also slower than mules at learning to find their way through mazes. At one time this led to the view that mules, like many other hybrids, are more intelligent than pure-bred equids (horses and donkeys). I once tried to find a test other than maze-learning by which the intelligence of mules and horses could be compared, but like Gillian Cooper, I found that the horses I studied had so many different ways of achieving their goals that their intelligence could not be compared. If, as seems to be the case, horses prefer to regard their own reflections in a mirror as living equine strangers rather than as images of themselves, is this really a sign of stupidity? As Gillian McCarthy wrote in one such case, she prefers to feel 'that any species which can lie down and roll over cattle grids (like Exmoor ponies) must be exhibiting intelligence.'[12]

Whatever the part played by intelligence in forming associations, the fact is that as these do become more and more firmly ingrained with each experience, so there is less and less need for consciousness to be involved in their performance. They become automatic, or as we commonly say 'reflex', actions, although such an everyday use of this term is not welcomed by physiologists for whom it has a special significance.

Associational training can be used to overcome quite a number of natural fears and phobias (see Chapter IV), but it must not be forgotten that a great deal of learning comes from gaining *experience* (e.g. going to different places, seeing and doing different things, trying out new skills or techniques), and even more from gaining an insight into how the things around us work and what has to be done to achieve certain ends.

The Effect of Mood

When introducing individuals to new experiences, it is important to ensure that their moods are adequate to, and will encourage, learning, for if the individual is too excited, apprehensive or worried, or not comfortable in his body, he may be distracted from paying full attention to the situation, and these heightened emotions and feelings will be all he associates with the experience in the future. In humans, sadness, anger or irritation aroused by a preceding (and perhaps quite unconnected) experience are often carried over into the riding session, to turn what should be an enjoyable period into one of moroseness and misery. Others let off their pent-up feelings by 'taking it out' on the horse, and so spoil for their mounts what should be a happy occasion. If a young and inexperienced rider comes to a first lesson expecting the worst (and perhaps thinking about all sorts of hair-raising stories he has been told about the sport), he is unlikely to give it his full attention. It is therefore a great help if riders of all ages and grades can be aware of their own moods before mounting and talk over their worries with an experienced colleague (or teacher), so ensuring that they are calm, and happily expectant before they even mount.

In a horse, an over-heating diet (or an over-full stomach) may well distract its attention from the lesson in hand and take its mind away from the point at issue. It must be remembered, however, that certain breeds of horse, such as Thoroughbreds, are more likely to be 'hyped up' by a heating diet than others, just as, in fact, they are naturally more physically active.

The loss of a leader or a trusted companion can be just as devastating to a horse as it is to a human, and can leave it in a state of despair and dejection until a replacement is found. In the foal this can start with weaning, when the trauma of

Expecting the worst

suddenly being separated from its mother – its mentor and protector until that moment – can be devastating. In *The Behaviour of Horses* (1987), Marthe Kiley-Worthington stresses this point very strongly, attributing many of the vices and abnormalities of behaviour seen in later life to this early bereavement.

Social Hierarchy

A few years ago, the concept of 'social hierarchies' in all animal societies was considered to be an important element in establishing harmony and order among horses. All fights between individuals were attributed to battles for position in rank order, and it was believed that a herd of wild horses was ruled over by a stallion (albeit through directing operations from the rear if the group was on the move), while the choice of food and resting area was left to the senior mare.

Nowadays this simple concept of a permanent and unalterable 1–2–3 ranking system has been somewhat modified to accept different grades and groupings according to the needs of the moment. In the 1980s it became more fashionable to believe that each individual takes up a certain attitude depending on the group it is with (and in the case of humans to whom one is speaking at a particular moment).

John Watson has outlined three different attitudes recognisable in most human societies:
1. Parental (loving, comforting, protective)
2. Adult (experienced, knowing, condescending)
3. Childish (begging, questioning, testing)

An individual adopting these attitudes will, in the first case, bend over and look down towards the person he is talking to, as if protecting that person; in the second case he will draw himself upright and stare straight ahead as if giving orders; while in the third will look up as if begging.[13]

Whether horse societies have quite the same system as this seems doubtful; but it is most probable that they can, and do, communicate with one another at various different levels.

PART III

The Prevention of Nervousness

CHAPTER IV

Maintaining Peace of Mind in Horses

The thoughtful management of horses – especially young ones – is of the greatest importance in preventing nervousness from developing. A number of factors are important in establishing equine peace of mind.

Companionship

The presence of one or more companions is essential for a contented mind in all naturally herd-living animals. However, where another horse is not available to keep a single horse company, an amazing variety of other creatures (and even objects) are frequently and successfully used to take its place. Stories of horses becoming inseparable from goats, donkeys, sheep, dogs and even chickens have been told, while soft music can also serve as a useful stand-in for live companionship. Among the commonest objects that have been used as substitute companions are large, soft balls, which can be kicked about and rolled along in the bedding.

The company of an experienced tutor – in the case of foals, preferably the dam – when exploring and investigating the world at large is the greatest help, but much will depend on the state of mind of the tutor, for while calmness is very reassuring, nothing is more infectious than 'vibes' of excitement, which are often given out (and received) without any conscious know-

A solitary horse will create a friend of any live companion

ledge on the part of the giver or receiver. Nowadays, gadgets are available that can measure and record these small electrical impulses; Joanne Jones has given a graphic account of her experience with one:

> A friend lent me her skin resistance meter to note my variations in tension. I was disappointed as it varied so slightly unless I was cold or pressed it hard in my hand. I tried it on the telephone when making a call in a state of 'aggro'. No difference. I telephoned someone I was really delighted to speak to. No change.
>
> Then I had a problem with a dog I had rescued. Out rabbiting the dog had met another dog and they had been seen with sheep. I

telephoned the farm manager, and learned from his wife that there would be a reprieve. I felt great relief, and as I replaced the telephone receiver I recalled the meter. It had gone right over the top of the reading zone. Two weeks later, out hacking on my rather hot young Thoroughbred, I met another farmer in the neighbourhood who I thought might have heard the dog story, and as we talked about it my horse exploded, plunged, snorted and rolled into a ball ... How I would have misunderstood him had I not remembered the meter experience.[1]

Another example, without the necessity of a skin resistance meter to demonstrate it, was reported by Mary Good:

Kesh, my Arab cross, had always been terrified of tractors, but I tolerated this short-coming believing it to be a genuine fear. When ridden out in company he was fairly good in normal traffic and hid behind the others when a tractor loomed on the horizon. When out alone, I knew all the safe places and gaps where we would retreat to until the monster had passed.

A short time ago I arranged for a contractor to cut the field hedges, making a mental note to move Kesh out of the fields concerned so he would not be upset by the tractor. However, the contractor came early and was noisily chopping and slicing through the hedge, branches and twigs flying everywhere – and where was Kesh? Grazing quite peacefully on the inside of the hedge, leaves and debris falling on him and only a few feet of hawthorn between him and the tractor on the road outside. I stood there for a few seconds, while the significance of this filtered through to my rather stunned brain. Had he been fooling me all these years?

Then he caught sight of me, flung his head up and galloped off, showing all the symptoms of having met a tractor unexpectedly. He tore round the field and by the time he eventually came to me he was covered in sweat and visibly shaking.

It's obvious to me now that it was my presence which triggered off his fright. He thinks I expect him to be frightened, therefore he is. I don't even have to be riding him for him to feel that way.[2]

To riders as well as to horses, the 'vibes' of nervousness are detectable and infectious. As parents are commonly – and naturally – apprehensive when their small children start riding for the first time, it is strongly recommended by the Association of British Riding Schools that the parents should not be involved in giving the first lessons. Indeed, one instructor went so far as to suggest to me that the best technique was to . . .

> get the parents out of the way altogether during the first lessons. The trouble is that they usually want to see some improvement in their child's performance every moment, and become critical if they do not. This tends to be discouraging and does not give the child time to practise one stage before going on to the next. An impartial outsider can be a great help here, and will usually recognise what a child is doing wrong without blaming him.[3]

For this reason too, it is recommended that first rides should be taken in groups; for among a group of children there is usually a sense of fun that can make a game out of a lesson and relieve tension. Pony Clubs do a great job here, and those who give up their time to run them deserve everybody's gratitude.

The infectiousness of nervous tension is one reason why a novice rider is never recommended to ride a novice horse at such potentially scaring events as horse shows, with their blaring loudspeakers, large vehicles slithering about on the grass, people shouting and strange horses going in all directions. In such a situation, an experienced mount will be far better company for an inexperienced rider than a novice one, and an experienced rider will help a novice horse to settle down and take in the importance of all that is going on around it for future use.

An experienced partner can also be very helpful in 'curing' his or her companion of established fears. It is not uncommon for a horse that has taken to shying at traffic or playing up in some other situation to be sent to an expert to reschool. After a week or so, the expert will often return the horse as cured – only for the trouble to reappear again when the original rider remounts. It must be assumed that it was not so much the *particular* situation (e.g. the passing cars) alone that triggered the behaviour as the *total* situation, including the rider's appre-

A novice rider is never recommended to ride a novice horse at horse shows

hension every time he or she saw a car approaching. For this reason, reschooling is often more successful if horse and rider are retrained together. Once a horse has confidence in its partner, it is staggering to see where it will go for him or her, even tackling some of the fiercest fences to be met with on cross-country courses.

Freedom

The need for freedom, and the improvements in behaviour resulting from it, have been graphically described by members of the EBSC. In 1986 Diane Harvey wrote: 'I took on loan a handsome 10 year old TB gelding, Apple ... His owners had kept him at a livery yard where he had received the best care and pampering but where he spent the vast majority of his time in his box, learning to crib bite. He also became a renowned bucker.' In Diane's hands, he spent all day and night out in the summer and at least five hours per day out in the winter, and after a little while he became . . .

sweet and quiet and the darling of the stable. I gradually realised that it was not my skill that had improved him but the hours of freedom he spent in the field . . . It is in the winter only, when he has to be stabled for longer, that I can see the origin of some of the rumours that had been spread about him. He gets jealous of his food and threatens when he is groomed or rugged up, and is inclined to nip. But as soon as the weather allows and his freedom is restored, you couldn't ask for a more genuine gentleman.[4]

Mrs Babs Elsworth followed this up by describing the behaviour of two horses owned by her and her husband: Rosie (a TB/Welsh cross), and Glen (Irish Draught). 'They are at a livery yard where day-time turn-out during the winter is not permitted . . . but during the summer they are out at grass all the time. Glen's only change during the winter months is that he becomes slightly more "edgy" to ride.'
But Rosie is a bit more erratic:

Her normal 'phobias' seem to be much more exaggerated during the winter. Tightening a surcingle always evokes the ears back reaction, but in the stabled months we get added clenched teeth and occasionally a head swung round as if to nip, though she never has. Ears back is again her reaction to a girth being tightened, but in winter she likes to take a grip of the top of her stable door with her teeth and grind them on it. Tummy grooming holds no problems in the summer but once stabled we get ears back, flicked tail and sometimes a defiant foot stamp. Her slight head-shyness becomes more pronounced when stabled. She's an excellent ride in traffic all year round and is always a 'lively' ride, but in winter seems to adopt an object to be frightened by for a few days before turning her attention to another item.[5]

Physical Exercise

All animals need to exercise their muscles regularly, but in animals such as horses, which have always depended for their existence on travelling long distances and the ability to outrun their enemies, the need to keep fit is particularly important. Horses that have to live in small, enclosed stables or yards for any length of time, will quickly resort to such vices as box-walking or weaving in order to work off some of their excess energy. Experimental studies to prove this point are not really needed, but in 1973 Deborah Street carried out a carefully controlled study for the California State Institute.[6] A twelve-year-old gelding, who was housed in a single corral and shelter, was ridden at walk and trot for one hour under the scrutiny of an observer, following none to four days without exercise.

The observer's task was to count the number of times the head was tossed, and the number of spooks or bucks during each period of riding. Not surprisingly, the number of these incidents corresponded to the length of time the horse had been confined and inactive. In addition to the number of incidents recorded, the rider noted very much quicker and more sudden spontaneous activity in the horse after prolonged rest.

The tendency for some horses to open their stable doors or jump out of their home fields was the subject of a group study undertaken in 1985 by members of the EBSC at the suggestion of the secretary, Gillian Cooper. Gillian asked all those members who had owned, or knew of, such escapologists to write and tell her (among other things) whether the animal jumped out for any apparent reason, what time of the year it did so, where it went after escaping, and what sort of a jumper it was under saddle. Her reason for suggesting the topic was because she suspected that most instances occurred in spring or autumn, 'harking back to some ancestral memory when wild herds would trek to different grazing, causing our domesticated horses and ponies to "follow the call" and go adventuring'. However,

> ... this proved to be nothing more than a romantic theory on my part. Out of 30 animals of which I have received details, only one yard involved spring/autumn escapes, and one animal only was a ring-leader.
>
> I had thought that, if horses broke out to go adventuring, they would naturally leave the home area and wander all over the neighbourhood. Again, only in one case did this happen. Most horses stayed close to home, some actually made for the stable yard after leaving the field where their companions were, one preferred human company to equine anyway, and one was impossibly greedy and knew that food was to be had in the stable yard – and this despite a well-grassed field.
>
> It was noticeable that all the 'jumper-outers' were good and usually willing jumpers under saddle. Although they would jump out to get to food (in the stable yard), other grazing or known and familiar company, none jumped out simply to meet strange horses passing by, despite showing interest where this was reported.
>
> Some who wandered off a little way were found grazing or snoozing on neighbouring lawns or common land ... However, most of the cases reported for this project stayed close to home and many actually jumped back again when fed up with exploring.[7]

The human need for physical exercise has been recognised for many years. In prisons, the exercise yard is an essential area, and many ex-prisoners-of-war have recalled that one of their few bearable moments was if their captors allowed them a wash down and a work-out. For many hard-working people the daily (or weekly) ride is the high spot of a busy life, and no efforts are too great to ensure that this is not spoiled by fear.

Associations with Pleasure

Associating all new or potentially frightening situations with something enjoyable – like food, verbal encouragement and praise, and also, in the case of horses, a gentle pat on the neck – can prevent nervousness ever developing. Soft music is also much appreciated by most horses, and can be used to soothe horses stabled alone if left to play on a tape recorder.

The use of food to accompany the presentation of normally fear-provoking procedures (such as coat-clipping with noisy electrical machines) has been used for many years by experi-

Soft music will soothe horses stabled alone if left to play on a tape recorder

enced horse-managers, and its value was also demonstrated by a group of researchers at the State University of New York. Seven horses of one- to three-years-old had their 'bridle-paths' (i.e. a line behind the ears and up and over behind the poll, where the bridle lies) clipped in a barn-aisle with a person holding the lead-rope, another operating the clippers, and a third observing and noting the number of head-tosses and movements of each horse. Before the test began, the horses had been randomly assigned to two groups. In one group, twice daily for 25 days, the clippers were switched on within earshot of the horses for ten minutes at the beginning of each feeding session, so that the horses could see and hear them as hay was distributed. In the other group, in addition to this, they were actually touched on the neck with the hand holding the clippers, so that they were exposed to the vibrations of the clippers as well as to the sound.

At the end of the treatment, all the horses were clipped again as on the first occasion, and the differences between the reactions of the two groups were noted. The information thus received indicated that the time spent on activating the clippers during the feeding period had been well worth while, although there was little statistical difference between the group that had felt the vibration of the clippers and the group that had only heard the sound.[8]

The importance to all animals – and especially horses – of associating enjoyment with obedience to *our* signals (e.g. the riding aids) was emphasised in Chapter III, but in the case of a horse, the importance to *it* of its rider being happy is just as great. The Pony Club (through the British Horse Society) recognises this and encourages the use of games as teaching instruments, just as the British Army encouraged acrobatics and musical rides in the days when the defence forces of the country were much dependent on cavalry and mounted regiments.

Verbal encouragement and praise liberally showered on pupils are far more effective than punishments and criticism, although gentle correction may be useful to improve riding technique.

The Importance of Smell

There is one more aid to tranquillity and/or pleasure that should be mentioned, namely the value of sweet odours.

Luckily for us, horses have much the same odour preferences as humans, and sweet-smelling flowers, hair sprays and aftershave lotions have all been used in the past to allay the fears of anxious equids. In fact, it has been suggested that the once-fashionable habit of well-dressed huntsmen wearing a bunch of violets in their button-holes was not really so much to attract the ladies as to dispel the apprehensions of their mounts by offsetting the smell of foxes or mud that might have accumulated on their clothes from previous outings.

I once met an old blacksmith who, if a strange horse was ridden into his yard, would smear his neck and collar with scent before going out to see to it, maintaining that this would allay any possible anxiety the horse might feel about having a stranger pick up and start cutting into its feet.

Conversely, the smell of fear in others (probably conveyed through sweat) is extremely infectious. Even humans, albeit subconsciously, are often aware of, and responsive to, this signal, but horses, with their much larger noses and more acute olfactory system, will detect it in minute quantities. Like many other liquids, sweat has a way of sticking to cloth, earth and even to the walls of buildings, and it is now believed that this is often the reason why many horses and some humans may have a sense of foreboding when in the proximity of anyone who has suffered, or in a place that has been the scene of suffering in the past.

CHAPTER V

Calming the Nerves

Drugs and tranquillisers which calm the nerves by reducing their ability to transmit electrical impulses have been known about and used for centuries. They come in a variety of different forms including gases; but do carry some dangers to the individual, in that they also reduce the acuteness of the sense organs and the functions of the brain as a whole. If taken in large quantities or over a prolonged period of time, they can affect the whole bodily system. Moreover, the return to full awareness after each intake is nearly always accompanied by an emotional swing in the opposite direction – i.e. depression – so the desire to repeat the intake and become re-intoxicated is extreme. In other words, they are addictive or habit-forming.

In the absence of outside assistance, the body will produce, and circulate, its own tranquillisers, the 'endorphins'; but, as already mentioned, the release of these depends on pressure at certain points on the skin. This, too, can quickly build up into a destructive habit – for example, in horses, that of crib-biting, and in humans of smoking or biting the nails.

Fortunately there are other, less drastic, ways in which nervous tension can be released and one of the most important is matching the diet to the amount of physical energy required for work on a day-to-day regime. The importance of this balance really cannot be overstressed.

All species of animal on a diet that is rich in vitamin content and contains much easily digested protein (which is readily absorbed by the blood) are likely to be 'jumpier' than those near starvation, who are barely able to keep their vital organs going.

There are also substances that lower the speed at which nervous impulses spread, and thus enable the individual to relax and 'feel good'. In humans, alcohol is frequently used for this purpose, while horse-food manufacturers and suppliers have many secret recipes for either energising slothful horses or calming 'jumpy' ones. Although many feed salesmen may overstress the efficiency of their products, no experienced horseman (or veterinary surgeon) would question the importance of a diet related to an individual's work needs.

In addition to the danger of overheating, the danger of underfeeding must be guarded against. The horse family is almost unique in its need for nearly continuous access to vegetation. Because of the shape of the horse's alimentary canal – a small stomach, in which the food is mixed with digestive juices, followed by a long intestine from which most of the absorption of nutrients into the bloodstream takes place – horses need to eat most of the time that they are not resting or moving. Unless they can see, or know that they can reach, hay or grass whenever they need it, they will be restless and ill at ease.

The horse's tendency to do a lot of eating at night and in the dark (when natural predators would not be able to see it so clearly) has been recognised for a long time, and the late night feed is one of the hardships that stable managers have had to learn to live with. Even after centuries of domestication, this tendency still persists, and those who have monitored a horse's intake over 24-hour periods have always remarked on how – whether stabled or at liberty – horses will munch away non-stop from midnight to dawn, and then stretch out on the ground until the sun is well up over the horizon.[1]

Horses at liberty are usually fairly adept at selecting those herbs that contain the substances their bodies most need at a particular time, and they will regulate their activity and water intake according to the diet available. Unfortunately, their

The horse's tendency to do a lot of eating at night and in the dark

innate sense of suitability is not always foolproof. Ragwort (*Senecio*), which has a toxic effect on the kidneys if eaten in any quantity, seems to be very appealing to certain strains of horse, particularly Arabs, as S. Marinier and A. Duncan demonstrated in a study extending over several years on a farm in South Africa.[2]

However, it is remarkable how horses that are stabled at night and turned out in the daytime will regulate their walking exercise according to the calorific content of their diet. Carol Yarwood was able to demonstrate this in a study she undertook for Wolverhampton Polytechnic College in 1985. By attaching a pedometer to a small harness, she correlated the total distance her horse travelled each day with a carefully regulated feeding programme and found that as the amount of protein increased, so did the movement recorded. Other factors, however, such as the surrounding temperature and relative humidity, also had some effect.[3]

Skin Care

The skin of all mammals is filled with nerve-endings that, if 'rubbed up the wrong way' can be irritated and become painful. Ill-fitting clothes, like breeches that ride up the leg and form lumps behind the knee, can put a person off riding for life. In the same way, ill-fitting tack on a horse can distract its attention and make it averse to the whole process of working with people.

However, it is not just during a ride that the skin needs attention. After a long, hard, sweaty grind (out hunting or during a race) the most comforting thing possible for all animals is a long, warm wash all over; before a good horseman will indulge himself in this way, he should always see that his horse has received the same attention.

Before setting out on a ride, it is just as important to ensure that a horse has been well groomed, so that sweat can reach the air and evaporate instead of collecting over the skin's surface.

Horses that are free in a field have their own ways of grooming themselves. Rubbing their necks or tails on posts, rails or tree trunks may comfort them, but can be very inconvenient for their owners. Rolling is another of their favourite pastimes, but exactly what purpose this serves has never been quite clear. Sheila Asker discussed the subject:

Popular belief seems to be that horses cover themselves in mud to keep warm – a natural instinct dating back to their days in the wild.

On reflection, this cannot be the case as when it is cold my mare's coat sticks up in order to trap air and keep her warm – a plastering of mud would surely defeat the object. It could be argued that a muddy horse is less conspicuous than a clean one and a grey, say, would blend into the background more easily if covered in mud, so it may be done for camouflage.

My mare Pandora has spates of rolling, whatever the temperature, and will then go for days without rolling and remain beautifully clean. I have never known her to roll when it is actually raining, nor is she particular about which sort of mud she chooses. I think horses tend to copy each other in this habit and have special rolling places. Even when the ground is dry she will sometimes seek out an oasis of gunge somewhere. This is usually in summer when I think it may be cooling and perhaps a relief from flies, etc. Sometimes she will roll immediately after being put out in the field after a ride, but not always. This could be due to itchiness after wearing a saddle for some time.[4]

One possibility is that rolling is a form of massaging the skin, which, as most people know, is a very good way of calming the nerves. For horses, a good grooming, coupled with a few minutes of old-fashioned 'strapping', i.e. banging the muscles on the neck and quarters with a handful of plaited straw or a folded cloth in rhythmical, sloping swings of the arm, probably has the same effect. Taking, long, deep, regular breaths at the same time as moving the shoulders upwards and backwards, is a good way for humans to relax the whole body and mind. As Richard Shrake has written:

Relaxation is critical to world-class performance in any sport. You may have seen this in watching Olympic or major league athletes warm up for their events ... they take deep breaths, deliberately stretch and loosen their muscles, and attempt to remove all tenseness from their bodies. In effect, they are trying to open the body's oxygen pathways to give it maximum fuel.[5]

A sense of tranquillity and invigoration is increased if the jaws are moved to and fro at the same time.

Let no one think I am suggesting that we should aim to replace lively, adventure-seeking, energetic animals with phlegmatic, listless, half-starved automatons, but the body and mind will only be able to give of their best and fulfil their natural potential if bursts of energetic output are alternated with periods of complete relaxation including periods of untroubled sleep.

PART IV

The Management of Fear

CHAPTER VI

Teaching the Nervous Rider

I am indebted to Lesley Young, BHSAI, who provided this chapter.

The Novice Adult

In recent years riding has boomed as a leisure activity and more and more adults from non-horsey families and backgrounds are now taking up the sport. Some of them may have ridden before, at trekking centres or perhaps as a child. Others may never even have been close to a horse, still less sat on one. For all of them, learning to ride properly is a new experience, requiring a great deal of physical effort, using muscles that are unfit, and involving some loss of adult dignity as they struggle to make a knowing horse do what they want it to while around them small children perform the same feats with ease.

Taking up riding is quite a challenge and sometimes the only things that keep the adult beginner going are perseverance and the tiniest glimmer of an idea that this just might be fun once they have got to grips with it. Naturally, they are nervous. They are nervous of falling off, of looking foolish, or of the horse falling over or 'bolting', and it is up to the teacher to make it all worthwhile for them.

The first few lessons that any novice has must be given in a one to one session with the teacher – there is no other way to ensure the safety of the pupil, nor to make certain that key information is being absorbed. This fact is equally true for both the adult and the child beginner.

Some loss of adult dignity

A nervous rider must be taught by an experienced teacher on a suitable horse, certainly for the first few months, otherwise they are unlikely to get over their nervousness. Anything else is a recipe for disaster. After they have stopped being so nervous, they could consider having lessons from a friend, but I would not recommend it unless the friend has teaching experience and the horse they are using is utterly reliable.

The first step is to introduce the rider to his or her mount. Obviously, this must be a safe, experienced, well-mannered horse that is accustomed to carrying novice riders. The pupil must be shown how to approach a horse with safety and how to touch it. He or she must be encouraged to speak to it and watch its reactions to everything around it. This is an excellent time to begin to impart a little horse psychology to the pupil. The teacher should explain why one should not walk straight up to a horse's face and try to touch its head, what sort of things worry a horse, how a horse sees, where its blind spots are and how it might well react to a sudden movement or an unpleasant noise close behind it. It is important that the novice should understand how nervous and easily startled any horse can be and know how to behave around a horse with safety. Once the rider understands why a horse reacts sharply to certain things, he is less likely to say to himself, 'This horse is dangerous,' than 'This horse is merely startled and I must help it to calm down by patting its neck and talking to it.'

This introductory session may take some time if the rider is nervous. It will help if the teacher is seen to be happy to stand close to the horse and to touch it. By encouraging the pupil to speak to the horse, the teacher can help to relieve the nervousness of tightened throat muscles and so help the nervous pupil to relax. Encourage the pupil to stroke the horse's neck and to experience how warm and soft the horse's skin is. Let him look into the horse's eye – the deep brown kindly eye of a calm horse is both beautiful and mesmerising, something frequently remarked on by people who have never been this close to a horse before.

Later sessions of this type can involve touching the horse's face and back, before teaching the necessary skills of handling the legs in safety and lifting up the feet to pick them out with a hoof pick. All novice riders, but especially nervous ones, should be taught how to touch a horse firmly and slowly. Nothing is more calculated to make a horse react restlessly than the quick, fluttering, tentative movements of a nervous handler.

Having been taught how to approach and introduce himself

to the horse and how to touch it and having been given advice on some of the things never to do with any horse, the next step is for the rider to lead it down the yard to the school where the riding lesson will take place. At a later date the pupil will be taught to lead in a head collar, but on the first few occasions the horse must be wearing a bridle.

Throughout everything that the novice is asked to do during the first lessons, it is important that the teacher remains close by, but not touching the horse (except when assisting the pupil to mount), unless this becomes necessary. It is essential that the pupil accepts right from the start that he or she is in charge of the horse and that no one else can be expected to 'make' the horse do things. When leading, the rider must tell the horse when to walk forward and when to stop, to stand still, etc. Only if something unexpected happens (for example, if the hunt suddenly comes clattering past, unsettling every horse in the yard) should the teacher take the horse from the pupil for reasons of safety, and even then the horse must be given back as soon as things have reverted to normal. The novice rider, especially the nervous one, must be made to dominate the new partnership from the outset.

Everything the rider is taught should be done in the proper way and the reason behind each particular action, i.e. running up stirrups, leading properly, etc. should be explained as you go along. Most things are done in a certain way for reasons of safety or to ensure the comfort of the horse. Once the new rider understands this, he is usually very careful about following the procedures he has been taught, provided that this is what he sees going on around him. If other riders are seen to employ sloppy or dangerous methods without rebuke, this is the example that will often be copied. However, do avoid telling a nervous beginner horror stories of horses that fell over going through the doorway into the school or panicked and reared up, throwing the rider off in a heap, just because stirrups were left dangling. This is not the time to terrify an already apprehensive novice.

Do avoid telling a nervous beginner horror stories

The first time a beginner sits on a horse's back and feels the horse shift about, he or she is bound to feel nervous and to clutch on with legs and hands. Do not rush the rider through this by bombarding him with instructions about holding the reins and the aids. In the case of a really nervous person, none of this information will sink in anyway. Instead, ask the rider how he feels, be sympathetic, agree that it takes a little getting used to and encourage him to take deep breaths and sit up and relax his legs. Frequently the novice rider feels he is sitting up straight when he is really leaning forward and is reluctant to bring his shoulders back for fear of falling off backwards. It is useful to hold an upright stick behind him at right angles to the saddle and ask him to lean back until he touches it so that he can feel the stick against his back when you tell him that he is now sitting straight.

Spend as much time as is needed accustoming the rider to the feel of the horse. Some people adapt very quickly, others feel very insecure and must be coaxed to shift about and move their legs and arms until they feel safer. Provide a neck strap or allow the pupil to keep the fingers of one hand lightly under the pommel of the saddle while he lets the other hand hang free. Ask him to change hands so that he becomes accustomed to moving his shoulders. Before adjusting the stirrup length, get the rider to stretch his legs down long and put his heels down. Encourage him to relax the leg rather than gripping with the knees and explain the importance of the body being soft and strong, rather than stiff and tense. Explain the correct position for the rider to adopt and try to give reasons for everything you ask him or her to do. A rider in the correct position is not only more effective but is also more in control and less likely to slip off than one who is tense or hunched forward.

Explain the aids for walk and halt before you ask the horse to move. Tell the rider where you are going to head for, i.e. to a letter marked out on the school wall or some other easily seen point. Then ask the rider to apply the aids and go forward in walk. At the first feeling of movement the nervous rider will instantly tense up again and clutch at the saddle. Do not worry him too much over his position; just keep the horse walking on and allow him time to relax. At all times during this procedure, the teacher must remain by the shoulder of the horse, holding it on a leading rein. When you reach the point allocated for halt, remind the pupil of the aids for halt and ask him to apply them. Once halted, it is time to adjust the rider's position and discuss his or her use of the aids. You may find that you have to repeat pieces of information several times over, especially with a very nervous rider as they often find it very difficult to concentrate on anything you are saying. Encourage the rider to relax and pat or talk to the horse before you repeat the exercise.

Once the rider has relaxed enough to sit up and take in what you are asking him to do, you can try a few exercises at halt. Encourage the rider to shrug his or her shoulders up and down or circle them backwards and forwards. Tell him to roll his head round in a circle from left to right and then from right to left. Get him to raise one hand up in the air and move it from in front of him round to the side, keeping it loose and flexing the fingers. Ask him to turn his upper body to each side and back to the front again, all the while taking deep breaths and sitting up tall, but not stiffly.

This early lesson should not take longer than half an hour, with extra time allowed for the handling procedure at the beginning and time allowed at the end for leading the horse back to its box. Any longer than this is very tiring for a beginner, who, even though he or she may be fit in other sports, is being asked to use muscles that are probably quite weak and will feel stiff the following day.

Most novice riders progress very quickly at this stage and some can even be ready to try a short trot at the end of their first lesson. However, it is important not to push a nervous rider too hard this early on. They will already have had to use up a great deal of energy just in overcoming their fear and it may take two or three sessions before they relax fully, even at halt. With the truly nervous beginner it is important to introduce only one 'insurmountable impossibility' at a time.

End the session on a good note, with praise and encouragement and a chat about how things went.

As the novice progresses he or she should be able to ride the horse off the lead rope while the teacher stands a little way off. Each lesson should begin by re-establishing what has been learned in the previous session before moving on to try something new. Be prepared to explain previously imparted information again, perhaps in a different way, just to make sure it has been taken in. Encourage the rider to talk to you about his or her worries, many of which will be groundless and can be dispelled quite easily. Others, however, may be real enough, for example, a fear of falling off.

Every rider is bound to fall off a horse sooner or later, but on the whole the novice rider does not so much fall off as slip off over one shoulder and is unlikely to be hurt if the school has a properly maintained surface. However, if work proceeds with care while the novice rider gains confidence and learns to relax, he or she is unlikely to come off in these very early stages so that by the time this actually occurs their increased confidence should ensure that it will not be such a momentous event. Naturally, it is especially important that the nervous beginner does not come off until he or she has stopped being nervous about many aspects of riding in general and can regard the fall as an isolated incident, not something that is going to happen every time they sit on a horse.

When a rider does come off the teacher must use his or her discretion about how to handle this event. If, as is most likely at this stage, the rider has simply slipped off and is completely unhurt, he should be encouraged to remount, but must not be forced to do so. It is better if he does remount, however, as this will often dispel the importance of the incident, providing the rest of the lesson continues without a problem. The teacher should talk about the fall and the reasons for it and should make light of the business of dusting the rider down and point out how astonished the horse is and that it was not the horse's fault, but the rider's own error or loss of balance and therefore something over which the rider has complete control and can prevent happening again.

If, however, the rider is completely wracked with fear about the fall, he or she should not be forced to remount, especially if the teacher feels the incident may recur. Nor should the pupil be made to feel either a coward or a failure, but it should be assumed cheerfully that things will go better in the next lesson. This next lesson will then be crucial in the relationship of teacher and rider. The teacher must use the session to restore confidence by working on exercises that the rider is well able to do before progressing further.

Obviously, if the rider seems dazed by the fall, or complains of pain, the lesson must be stopped and appropriate action taken.

The rider should not be forced to remount

A nervous, tense rider should not be introduced to canter until the teacher feels he or she is competent in trot without stirrups and that there is some sense of balance. Cantering often produces nervousness, making the rider grip up with the knees and increasing the chances of a fall. It is a good idea if the teacher demonstrates canter first and discusses the movement of the horse as well as the aids for canter, to prepare the pupil for this change of gait. Do not go on and on cantering in the first few sessions; do a short amount in the middle of the lesson and then work in trot on exercises that the pupil can cope with easily, thus ending on a good note.

As the rider improves, he or she may be able to join a group of novice adult riders. This can be most enjoyable and can do a lot for the confidence of a nervous rider as he sees the efforts, mistakes and successes of his companions. Frequently riders in a group will try harder in order to do as well as their companions and progress can speed up. However, it is vital that the teacher remains aware of the fact that one or more of the members of the class is nervous and does not overface them or put them in situations where they will be made to feel small or ridiculous. Within a group, riders are far less likely to voice their worries for fear of losing face, and it is up to the teacher to be on the alert for signs of anxiety or unhappiness.

Teaching the Elderly or Disabled Novice

The greatest fear of an elderly novice rider is of falling off and in this case it is a real worry and should be recognised as such by the teacher. While the average-fit adult is unlikely to suffer much more than bruised dignity at this early stage, an elderly or disabled person can suffer lasting physical damage. It is essential in this situation that teaching remains on a one to one basis and that lessons remain short and not too strenuous. The teacher must watch for signs of cramp and physical discomfort as well as nervousness and must also be prepared to progress slowly and very steadily. An elderly or disabled rider does not have the same strength in his muscles as a younger fitter rider and his bones may well be much more brittle and liable to break in a fall.

Teaching the Nervous Child

Unlike adult novices, children have not usually chosen to learn to ride because it is something they have always wanted to try. Riding is more often just one of a range of activities that they are involved in, like dancing, music lessons or swimming. Quite often, a child has no idea what to expect riding to be like, but young novice children frequently regard ponies as a cross between a furry living toy and a cuddly pet – unfortunately, so do many parents who have had no riding experience themselves. This attitude can lead to dismay and nervousness when the child first discovers that even the sweetest-natured pony is considerably stronger than he or she expected and that ponies do not obey commands like a trained dog.

Some children are nervous of the size of the pony, others fear it will stand on their feet, bite them or push them over. Once mounted, they fear the pony will run off with them or that they will fall off. It is at this point that the teacher must ensure that any child, but especially a nervous one, learns to handle and take charge of a quiet, 'bomb-proof', willing, honest, mature pony. Only by association with such a paragon of all virtue will the nervous child begin to overcome his or her fears and start to look on the pony as a friend that can be trusted. Indeed, should such a pony ever do anything out of character at a later date, far from becoming afraid and demanding to dismount, the once-nervous child will often assure you that whatever happened was not the pony's fault and may even see himself in the role of protector of his friend.

Any novice child, but especially a nervous one, must be taught in a one to one situation with an experienced teacher. Children are often brought for their first riding lessons at a very early age, before their physical co-ordination or powers of understanding are adequate. Obviously, some children develop at a different rate to others, but the age of seven seems to be about right in terms of ability and powers of understanding. It is important that the child can both communicate with his teacher and also understand what he is being told.

As with the adult novice, the child should be taught how to approach and handle a pony safely, and no child should ever be left alone with a loose pony or with one tied up in a confined space until the teacher is convinced that the safety rules are thoroughly understood. Unlike adults, children frequently become carried away by excitement and can easily forget what they have been told many times not to do, such as running across the yard, walking up behind a horse or stroking it in inappropriate places such as under the tummy or around the hocks.

Touching the pony is important for children, who will enjoy stroking their new friend. It is also a good idea to teach the child how to brush the pony safely and properly, again under supervision.

The first riding lesson must be given on a leading rein, both to ensure the safety of the rider and to calm the fears of the anxious parents. It is best to keep the parents at a distance during all lessons, either watching from a gallery or outside the rails of the school, or, even better, sitting in their car reading a newspaper, but this may not always be possible with a very nervous child. If the teacher thinks it necessary, on the first occasion one parent may be asked to stand on the other side of the pony to give reassurance by his or her presence. It is important, however, that the parent does not attempt to teach the lesson and that the teacher is the only person giving instructions and therefore holding the child's concentration. This is a situation that can require enormous tact on the part of the teacher and as soon as possible the parent should retire to the sidelines.

It is obvious that a child cannot be taught using the same language as an adult rider, so an explanation of the aids and position must be couched in words that the child can understand. Most children, especially in a new and scary situation, become very quiet and are unlikely to ask questions or voice their fears. It is up to the teacher to persuade the child to talk, to ask questions that will reveal whether or not the lesson is being understood and to spot the signs that will show how the child is feeling. A child who sits completely still, clutching the saddle with both hands, stares downwards and appears to be deaf, is scared. One who trembles or even begins to cry silently is terrified. Providing that the pony is standing quite still, however, there is no reason to take the child off, but the lesson cannot proceed until the child has relaxed. This is done by talking quietly and smiling and also by the teacher's touch. The teacher can hold the child's hand or merely cover it with her own if it is clenched tightly on the rein or saddle. This is comforting to a small child who is used to holding hands with friends and parents and who may then relax. The teacher can also place an arm lightly round the child's body, so that the child feels less insecure, or even give a reassuring hug. The teacher can try to get a two-way conversation going by offering information such as the pony's age and then asking the child what his age is, saying what the pony had for breakfast and then asking what the child had for his breakfast and so on. Even if there is no response, the teacher can continue a steady flow of chat in a kind voice. It is astonishing the number of times when one has almost exhausted one's store of trivia that a child will suddenly volunteer something about the family pet or a little brother or sister.

Now the lesson can proceed, but very slowly. Try to persuade the child to hold the reins, no matter how loosely, along with the pommel or a neck strap. This does give him or her more of an impression of being in the driving seat. Explain the aids for walk and halt and where halt will take place.

This is a good way to get the child to look up and around. Make sure the child has understood the words you have used. There is no point in saying, 'We are going to stop at the jump stand', if the child does not know what this is. Expect that signs of nervousness will return when the pony first begins to walk on, and maintain your conversation. If you feel that the child is so tense that he or she is likely to slip off the other side of the pony, ask an assistant to come in and help you. Every time you go forward to halt you can ask the child to wave to his parent and smile. This will help to relax the arms and face muscles and will free one hand from the saddle or neck strap.

After a bit of walking, try a few simple exercises to loosen the tension in the body. Circling one arm backwards and forwards and turning the shoulders and upper body from side to side should help. Do not expect the child to do anything advanced at this stage, like 'round the world', as this could make him dizzy if he is really scared and not breathing deeply. Some children tend to hold their breath if they are scared, so encourage conversation to prevent this.

Keep this first session short. If the child has been very nervous, he or she will be very tired by the end of half an hour. Give lots of praise and encourage the child to pat the pony and thank it for a nice ride. Assure the parents that it is better to progress slowly at this stage.

A nervous child novice should remain on a one to one basis with the teacher until he can walk, trot, canter and halt on either rein without anxiety. Introduce canter with care and make sure the child has seen someone cantering before he is asked to do it, in case he assumes he is being run off with. Canter for short periods and in the middle of the lesson before the child is too tired to use his legs effectively. If possible keep the child on the same pony for all the early lessons as this is often instrumental in building confidence. After a time other ponies can be tried, but be careful never to overface the child and make each first lesson on a new pony a successful one.

At some point the child may fall off through loss of balance. On a good school surface he is unlikely to be hurt, but will probably be both surprised and embarrassed and this may lead to tears. Unless you feel the child is hurt, encourage him to remount, but do not force him if he refuses. Dust the child down and try to make a joke out of the event. Tell the child about a time when you fell off and landed in a puddle and assure him that you were not hurt. Point out to the child that the pony is very surprised by this turn of events and encourage the child to pat and comfort it. If the child still does not want to remount, even to make the pony feel better, this may be a time to practice a bit of leading, turning and halting the pony, running up stirrups and loosening the girth.

When the child has reached a certain level of proficiency in walk, trot and canter, he or she may well enjoy the company of a group lesson. Again, try to keep the child on a pony he or she is used to and is relaxed enough with to be able to join a group. In a group situation each child receives less of the teacher's attention and the teacher must be aware of how each pupil is feeling without waiting to be told. Few children will risk the scorn of their peer group by saying that they are scared to do something and it is up to the teacher to know when to push, when to cajole and when to change the exercise to something that will restore the confidence of the least able or most nervous rider in the group.

Watch for signs of reluctance to get on with the lesson. These

Watch for signs of reluctance

are often an indication of anxiety or fear. Endless complaints
that stirrups are not even, that girths need tightening, of sore
fingers, headaches or pains in the tummy that appear immediately the class is asked to work without stirrups or to canter or
jump may or may not be what they seem. Such delaying tactics
can disrupt the whole class if allowed to continue and it is
important to keep the work of the rest of the group going while
you deal with the complainant. Obviously, pain cannot be
ignored and this child should be invited to sit quietly and watch
the rest of the class work. As the work proceeds, invite the
child to join in, but do not force the issue, nor pay too much
attention and thus neglect the rest of the pupils. If the pain does
not go away within a few minutes, then the child should
dismount and leave the lesson under the supervision of an
assistant who will keep an eye on him until his parent arrives. If
this sort of incident recurs, then a quiet word with the parents
is called for and it may be that the child should return to a one
to one teaching situation or be put in a class that is less
challenging.

Most children are nervous when faced with a new experience
and the advice given above is only for the exceptional child
whose nervousness is acute. The majority of children are very
willing to have a go and respond well to firm, persuasive
teaching. Having been reluctant to try something initially, they
then bounce with pride when a new goal is reached.

Humour is one of the teacher's greatest assets in working
with children, especially nervous ones. Everyone learns more
when they are having fun and many children try their hardest
when lessons also take the form of games. Try to incorporate
some simple gymkhana games into the classes from time to
time, such as egg and spoon races, walking up and trotting back
or statues. If these are done in a semi-official way at, say,
Christmas, rosettes can be given out. Try to arrange for everyone to receive some sort of prize. It is the greatest confidence-
booster in the world for a nervous child to take home a
colourful rosette.

There is a great difference between nervous anticipation before a lesson, that dissolves into chatter and laughter by the end, and sheer dread that leaves a child still miserable and tearful by the middle or end of every session. Learning to ride is not a matter of life or death and if the teacher feels that the child is genuinely afraid and unhappy, then it is time to speak to the parents. Rather than making the child feel he or she has failed at something, it is often a good idea for the parents to pick a suitable reason for stopping riding for a while – during granny's visit, until your cold gets better, while the days are so hot/cold – and leave the date of returning to the class open. If the child really does wish to go on with his riding lessons, he will ask to do so sooner or later. If he doesn't then matters are best left as they are. The child can always try again in a few years if he or she wishes to.

Specific Fears

For the nervous novice rider, both adult and child, everything to do with the horse is a source of worry, but frequently their nervousness wears off simply through association with a friendly and well-behaved mount. Once a rider is established in the basic skills, however, individual factors can still cause great nervousness.

HACKING

When any horse is taken out of the safe confines of an indoor or outdoor school and hacked out along the roads and through open spaces, it is liable to be more alert and on its toes, especially in blustery or frosty weather. Hacking out is fun and a relaxation for both horse and rider after the hard repetitive work of the school, but it also offers unpredictable moments – when a huge lorry appears round a bend, when a paper bag blows out of the hedge, when a woman comes along pushing a pram; for a split second even the quietest horse will regard all of these things as a potential danger and most horses will take a look at them before going quietly on. Out on the roads the nervous rider worries about traffic and the horse shying; in open spaces he or she may worry about the horse galloping off or tripping up. To the very nervous rider, every time the horse shakes its head at flies, this is a sure sign of things getting out of control.

A rider who is nervous of hacking must be taken out on a horse that is virtually 'bomb proof', accompanied by an instructor who is mounted on something equally quiet – not a recently backed four-year-old that needs exercising – and who is carrying a lead rope. For the first few times out of doors, it is a good idea to put a nervous child's pony on the lead rope, although the child must be made to ride the pony and not just sit as a passenger, being led about. For this reason, take the child off the lead rope as soon as you consider it safe to do so, and make the child take charge of the pony. Pick a route that is quiet and as traffic free as possible. Assure the rider that the horse knows the route well and is not afraid of tractors or any other obstacle you are likely to meet. Encourage the rider to relax his or her hands so that the horse is free to move its head and look around it. Advise the rider when something scary is coming up, like a black plastic bag. Warn him that the horse may look at it and may even stop, but that he must urge the horse forward, pat it, talk to it and praise it.

This is a good time to explain to the rider how the horse sees the outside world, what sort of fears the horse itself has – tigers, snakes, deep holes, things passing by too close and at speed. Explain that the horse is not playing up or being naughty, and is only in need of firm riding and reassurance from a calm rider. Try to make the rider understand that he must remain calm in all situations so that his nervousness will not communicate itself to the horse. Show the rider how to slow down traffic that is approaching too quickly.

A rider who is nervous of being unable to stop should not canter out of doors until he is relaxed about the idea of hacking out in general. The first canter should be in the company of one other well-behaved horse along a short strip of good ground or up a slight slope. It should not be in the company of several people racing along out of control nor heading towards a road. Explain the slightly forward position to adopt in canter and make sure the rider's stirrups are short enough to enable him to keep his legs underneath him. Tell him where you intend to begin the canter and where you intend to stop and also how to stop. It is a good idea to let him be the one to strike off first into canter and the first to pull up, as this gives a feeling of being in control. Don't overdo things on the first few rides. When the rider is happy with these outings, introduce longer canters, but make sure that these remain controlled. Sometimes let the rider go in front, sometimes give him a lead, but do not race. Always canter on ground that you know well and warn the rider of any point where the horse might swerve, such as by a dip in the ground, a tree stump, etc.

JUMPING

Jumping creates nerves in most riders, even those who enjoy it and do it well, so it is not unnatural that learning to jump can make otherwise confident riders anxious. It is important that the first jumping lesson is based on a firm understanding of the jumping position and the way the horse moves when it jumps. The nervous pupil should be encouraged to watch other people jumping over small fences, noting first how the rider adapts his position and then how the horse takes off and lands and especially how it rounds its back and stretches its neck in the air.

Work in jumping position and over trotting poles will help to improve the rider's balance, but nothing really prepares him for the first jump and it is important that this should be over a low jump, out of trot, with the rider holding on to a neck strap to avoid jabbing the horse in the mouth or losing balance. At first, keep the fences low and use a horse that is unlikely to stop or run out. Retain the neck strap for as long as you think necessary and always use a placing pole so that the horse takes off when the rider expects it to.

Most people will fall off at some point when learning to jump, but this usually follows a refusal or run out because the rider has dropped the horse in front of the fence, and therefore the fall usually happens quite slowly and painlessly. However, this sort of incident can become a vicious circle – the rider is nervous of falling off again and so tenses up and drops the horse which then runs out or refuses and the rider falls off again. With a rider who is nervous of jumping anyway, there is no point in going on and creating this hang-up. The teacher must explain the reason carefully to the rider and if necessary demonstrate that the horse can indeed jump that fence and that it is not too high or too difficult for it. If necessary, go back to an earlier stage of the training until confidence is restored.

A common result of nervousness – even among experienced riders – is to tense up the arms and body when turning towards a jump, thereby holding the horse's head up in the air so that it can no longer see the fence or balance itself for the leap. This causes many horses to lose their own confidence in jumping and to begin refusing or napping. Sabrina Benson, who specialises in dealing with nervous riders, recommends that such riders should be encouraged to hold the reins on the outside of the hand (instead of the inside, which is the usual position) so that when the riders pull their hands in towards their own bodies, the reins can slip loose and the horse is free to stretch its neck, can see where it is going and will not be jabbed in the mouth.[1]

Keep the jumps low and the sessions short, always ending on success so that the rider begins to feel that he or she can cope with this new skill. Progress slowly as it is vitally important when learning to jump that the nervous rider believes the teacher will never ask him to do something that he cannot do or that will cause him to be hurt. Once this trust is broken, it takes a lot of rebuilding.

At the end of the day, people learn to ride for different

reasons. Some just want to hack out, others to do simple dressage tests, some to hunt and some to compete at Badminton or win the individual gold medal for show jumping at the next Olympic Games. Find out what your pupils' ambitions are and do not push them beyond their limitations or into disciplines they do not want to try. Make riding fun for them and be content with slow progress providing the pupils are enjoying what they do and are growing in confidence. Lots of people have ended up taking part in gymkhanas when they only ever intended to hack out at weekends, simply because they overcame their own nervousness through the enjoyment of riding safely.

CHAPTER VII

Calming the Human Mind

Unfortunately, some people are so nervous of horses that they are unable even to approach one and are therefore unable to overcome their fear as described in Chapter VI. In order to understand their fear and begin to combat it, these people must seek specialised help. Perhaps the commonest cause of fear, in both horses and riders, is an awareness of fear in their companion. Thus, a nervous horse can arouse tension (and worry) in even the most confident of riders, and vice versa.

There are several methods for dealing with established fears in humans. These are described only briefly here, so that the reader may form an opinion as to the method he or she would prefer, and can even try it out briefly on themselves, although such treatment is best undertaken under expert supervision.

Habituation and Conditioning

Habituation, as its name suggests, consists of getting a person used to the fear-arousing situation and thus discovering it to be harmless. For this to work, the stimulus (or situation) is reduced to a minimum, but all means of escaping from it are blocked. The person is then kept in that situation until all the physical signs of fear (raised heart and breathing rate, shivering and skin tension) have ceased; then the next step (a more severe form of the situation) can be taken. For example, for a general fear of horses, the 'subject' (as the person undergoing the

Some people are so nervous of horses that they are unable even to approach one

treatment will be called) imagines a horse in the vicinity and then thinks of himself gradually approaching it.

As soon as he feels his tension returning, he should stop, take several deep breaths to relax his body, and then repeat the manoeuvre; and continue doing this until he can imagine himself close enough to smell and touch the horse without tensing up.

After several hours of rest, the 'treatment session' can be repeated until the person feels confident enough in his imagination to try it out in reality. At the first sign of fear, further progress forward should be halted. The subject should then return to the process of only imagining the horse, and when calmness is restored he may try repeating the procedure. It is helpful to measure the time taken from *exp*osure to *com*posure at each trial. If the treatment is succeeding, this recovery time will gradually diminish. Once it has reached zero, the next step – mounting or handling the real horse – can be taken, as described in Chapter VI.

Behaviour Therapy

A more concentrated form of habituation is known as behaviour therapy or conditioning, which, under its best known exponent, the Russian physiologist Pavlov, came to acquire rather a bad reputation. In a laboratory where everything could be carefully monitored and controlled, Pavlov's team were able to demonstrate that individual animals could, after only a few months of this treatment, be conditioned to live for the rest of their lives in a manner in which their natural parents and siblings do not. In the small carnivores in which this was demonstrated (rats and mice), rewards were provided in the shape of small quantities of food every time the required act was performed, and punishments, in the shape of electric shocks, were given for all other acts. For instance, the required act might be to stand on the hindlegs and press a lever. After this had been done, a small pellet of food would drop at the animal's feet. If it attempted to touch food presented in any other way, it received an electric shock. If the training programme was started early enough in the animal's life, and carried out intensively enough, it would affect its behaviour ever afterwards; even if freed and returned to its natural surroundings and community, the treated animal would be prepared to starve to death rather than break the trained habit.

Hypnotism

Training and re-training are not the only means by which fear and nervousness can be held in check. The value of hypnotism for this purpose was demonstrated in Paris in the late eighteenth and early nineteenth centuries by the German physician Mesmer, but has probably been used by many different kinds of animals (and certainly by different races of people under different names) since the beginning of life on earth. Some species of reptile (snakes, for instance) utilise its effects to paralyse their prey and prevent it from escaping.

The secret seems to be to attract one of the five senses (usually vision, but hearing and touch can be used as well) and make the body sway up and down or to and fro, or the breathing flow in and out in a slow, gentle regular rhythm until this movement takes over all the senses and the individual relaxes into a sleep-like state. The snake does this by lifting its own head off the ground and waving it from side to side. Once the prey starts following the movement with its own eyes, a sense of relaxation akin to sleep takes over the rest of the body. When the victim has been immobilised in this way, the predator can strike.

In the case of humans, the subject/patient is usually given an order to relax his body by means of deep breathing, closing his senses to everything except the hypnotist's voice and commands. The hypnotist may then chant something along the lines of, 'You are going to sleep now. Your arms are feeling numb; your head is dropping forward; your eyes are closing;

Fear and nervousness can be held in check by hypnotism

you are breathing deeply and slowly. You cannot feel your body. You are aware of nothing except my voice. You are happy and relaxed.' He will then tell the patient to carry out some act after he wakes (for example, 'Go and pat a horse on its neck and *enjoy* the feeling') but to forget everything that has gone on during the session, so that when the patient comes to carry out the act, he will think he is doing it of his own free will.

However, it is not essential for a person to be in a hypnotic trance for suggestion to have an important effect. Dr T. R. Roberts clarifies this:

> The crucial thing appears to be the relationship between the 'therapist' and the patient. A certain degree of friendly warmth and mutual trust is essential. With some people this comes very quickly, particularly if the subject is suffering stress. With others it seems to me to be so difficult as hardly to be worth the effort.
>
> My first step is to get the 'patient' to confirm the recognition of

some motivation or incentive-to-change. I suspect that this is crucial, and I see no point in proceeding without it. I then look for the patient's initial reaction when first exposed to the situation that gives rise to the stress. This is quite a difficult stage, as usually the patient does not realise that he is entering the condition in which the stress is going to arise. He only recognises the later stages when he is already conscious of stress of disturbing intensity. By that time in the sequence, it is far too late for the patient to be able to alter the way he is behaving. It is essential to find the 'trigger situation'.

My strategy is to get the patient to recognise the imminence of the stress-arousing situation, as a sort of 'aura' to which he becomes alerted. This has to be a picture of the situation in the early stages of its development, before he has actually begun to feel seriously affected. One can then try to devise a sequence of ideas about the situation that will lead the patient to a realisation that the stress is not inevitable, and also a realisation that he is perfectly capable of handling the situation without 'going over the edge'. The patient is encouraged to learn and rehearse this sequence of ideas.

The next stage is to train the patient to recall the sequence of calming reasoning as soon as he gets the first hint that a stress-generating situation is about to develop, and talk himself through it. The process is powerfully self-rewarding.[1]

Dr Roberts further suggests that as a rider becomes more confident and begins to enjoy riding, he may start to become more and more adventurous.

Whether such control can take place over a distance (that is to say, when the hypnotist and the patient are separated by either time or space, or both) has not been satisfactorily proved as yet, although many claims have been made that 'thought transference' can occur over vast distances. Claims have also been made that human thoughts can be transmitted to, and used to control, the behaviour of animals (and vice versa). One exponent of this idea was Henry Blake, a founder member of the EBSC. A keen horseman and an experienced scientist, Blake carried out many experiments on his own horses, including some he designed to test the ability of one horse to sense what was happening to another that it could neither see nor hear.[2]

Unfortunately, Blake's experiments (or modifications of them) are difficult to carry out and it has gradually come to be accepted that, as in the case of Clever Hans (see Chapter V), most cases of thought transference are due to the unconscious giving and receiving of body language signals.

If humans can pacify animals by exhibiting their own emotional calm, animals can also have this effect on humans. The pacifying and calming effect of a horse's presence on some mentally and physically handicapped people has been demonstrated (and measured) by scientific instruments. E. Royds described how electroencephalograph (EEG) readings were taken (by means of electrodes attached to the scalps of the subjects) from two children while horses were led into an area where the children could see and touch them. He reported that both children grew calmer in the presence of the horses than they had been before, and in one of them – who was also allowed to ride a horse – the increased calmness was particularly noticeable.[3]

Riding therapy for all types of disability is now in common usage, and one therapist described to me how a pupil of hers, who had grown up without any voluntary control over his legs at all, showed his first movements in them while sitting on the back of a pony, later on becoming able to walk.[4] Grooming ponies can also be helpful in such cases, while speech can be encouraged by getting children to name parts of their ponies and pieces of riding tack, etc., in circumstances where no sense of ridicule is attached to failure.

Psychoanalysis

When the dangers of 'handing yourself over to another person' (via behaviour therapy or hypnotism) came to be suspected, the fashion of teaching people how to help themselves developed. Sigmund Freud was one of the first to do this after studying hypnotism in Paris, where he became appalled at the idea that the so-called 'cured' patient might lose his free will and become an automaton under the control of the therapist. Freud's technique concentrated on teaching the patient to be his or her own therapist. The patient was simply told to lie down on a comfortable bed or sofa, relax his body, clear his mind, and utter the first words that came to him – especially those relating to any past experiences. Freud was impressed by the number of times his male patients mentioned a fear of horses, a fear that was never voiced by his female patients. He published one such case, and thereby evoked a mass of criticism. According to Alan Kazdin:

Hans, a five-year-old boy, feared being bitten by horses and seeing horses fall down. Freud believed that Hans's fear and fantasies were symbolic of important psychological processes and conflicts, including Hans's attraction toward his mother, a wish for his father's demise, and fear of his father's retaliation (i.e. the Oedipus complex). The case of Little Hans was considered by Freud to provide support for his views about child sexuality and the connection between intrapsychic processes and symptom formation.[5]

Because of these beliefs, two of Freud's early assistants later became his most hostile critics, setting up their own 'schools' of psychoanalysis, albeit along very similar lines to Freud. These men were Karl Gustav Jung and Alfred Adler. Jung believed that the 'memories' described by patients under analysis were those common to all people of a certain race (a 'collective unconscious'), and that the importance of horses in this was due to the important part that these animals had played in people's successes in the Western world. For Jung, the horse was a symbol of heroism in battle.

Adler, on the other hand, believed that the notion that he was master of all he surveyed, and that he could control everything around him was basic to man's contentment: he hated to admit that his horse was carrying *him* rather than the other way around. Women, on the other hand, being born without this need for dominance and supremacy, were only too glad to yield to a horse and felt 'uplifted' by its assistance.

All psychoanalysts agree that patients should be allowed, and encouraged, to find out these hidden truths for themselves. Instead of having their minds organised and controlled by the therapist, all that a modern analyst does is sit silently in the background, if necessary urging the patient to go on delving up ideas for himself, bringing them into the light, and looking at them critically. This process is often helped by patients being treated in groups, so that an idea or memory that has been publicly related by one can act as a cue to other members of the group and help them to excavate their own 'memory banks'.

There are many cases on record of horse phobias in people being cured on the analyst's couch, and of patients being able to enter stables and actually touch horses after treatment, when they could not even look at one before without trembling. As yet, I have not heard of anyone actually losing their fear of riding by this method, but if a person can learn how to relax (by deep breathing, slowly rotating the neck and shoulders, and moving the head from side to side) while in the saddle as well as on the ground, he or she may come to enjoy experiences which previously filled them with dread.

The opposite situation – that of a person being put on a horse, finding he can control it and *then* becoming capable of coping with many other problems (i.e. riding therapy) has already been stressed. E. Royds, one of the first people to hear an autistic boy uttering his first words while sitting astride a pony, went on to help found and manage the Riding for the Disabled movement.

The value of this and the process by which it can be achieved have been described by John Anthony Davies in his book, *The Reins of Life* (1988), which he introduces with the following lovely poem:

I Saw a Child

I saw a child who couldn't walk
Sit on a horse, laugh and talk.
Then ride it through a field of daisies
And yet he could not walk unaided.
I saw a child no legs below
Sit on a horse and make it go
Through wood of green and places he had never been
To sit and stare, except from a chair.
I saw a child who could only crawl
Mount a horse and sit up tall;
Then put it through degrees of paces
And laugh at the wonder on our faces.
I saw a child born into strife,
Take up and hold the reins of life
And that same child was heard to say,
'Thank God for showing me the way'.

John Anthony Davies[6]

CHAPTER VIII

Establishing Co-operation between Horse and Rider

Establishing co-operation between a horse and its rider involves two very important processes:

1. Each one learning the meaning of the other's signals;
2. Each one being prepared to adjust or alter their own behaviour to obey such signals.

The means by which humans have taught their own signals (the 'aids') to horses have been so varied and intricate that it would be impossible to describe them all, but basically all involve the horse in learning to associate a sight, sound, or touch with what its rider wishes it to do, and also learning that obeying these signals will bring it greater rewards than the opposite.

A horse's first task is to overcome its inborn fear of human proximity. Traditionally, the American horseman (or cowboy) did this by making the horse too exhausted to run away from him any more, by breaking its spirit or 'breaking it in'. First he would pull the horse to the ground by means of a lasso, then tie its feet together to prevent it moving while the saddle and bridle were fitted and the rider got ready to leap on its back, and finally letting it gallop off into the prairie until all its strength had evaporated and its resistance to its rider's demands were reduced to nothing. After this, it was comforted by means of gentle grooming and feeding – and it was hoped that these last two experiences would be the only associations with men that it would retain.

Not all Americans, however, used such apparently brutal methods as the traditional cowboy. One famous trainer, J. S. Rarey, who was born near Ohio in 1827, came to England and demonstrated, first to Queen Victoria in 1858 and then all over the country, how he could make even the most 'vicious' horses lie down on the ground beside him after spending only a few minutes alone with them in a small, enclosed space. Rarey's method

... was to use two straps to lift the horse's front feet off the ground, one at a time. Once the horse had been forced into a kneeling position, Rarey would gently but steadily exert enough pressure, either by leaning on the horse's shoulder, or by pulling on the strap attached to the off foreleg, to bring the horse down. The horse could either fall towards him or away from him and it was part of Rarey's skill to anticipate the horse's movements, so that the horse would lie down in the most comfortable position... While the horse lay helpless at his feet, Rarey would smooth and massage every part of its body until the muscles were relaxed and the horse was calm ... When Rarey took off the straps and told the horse to get up, it showed such confidence in him that it would follow him round the ring, or allow him to ride it, guided only by the lift of a hand even if it had never been ridden before.[1]

For some time Rarey was thought to be unique and believed to have used some secret soporific. It is now accepted, however, that horses can be habituated to a human presence – and to wearing the necessary tackle to carry a rider, and even to being mounted by one – without any use of force and in a remarkably short time. Monty Roberts, another American, who visited Britain in 1989 and gave demonstrations all over England – starting at Windsor Castle in front of HM Queen Elizabeth – used an 'approach and retreat' method by which he approached when the horse looked interested and expectant, and retreated as soon as it showed any fear or apprehension. If the horse is confined – as in his demonstrations – in a small corral to prevent its escape, the whole process of tacking up and mounting can be carried out in a very short time – in Monty Roberts's demonstrations this period was just about one hour.[2]

Most European horse trainers, however, feel that speeding up the process is not an advantage, but that time should be allowed for each stage to 'sink in' and become truly absorbed before the next is attempted. If this is not done and something goes wrong at a later stage, the whole process may have to be repeated all over again. There is the additional danger that if what went wrong was associated with pain or discomfort, the displeasure this aroused will be associated in the horse's memory with all later learning stages.

It is for this reason that most trainers are willing to take their time, first getting a horse completely used to a human presence and ensuring that this is associated with pleasant sensations (a soothing voice, a sweet smell or a handful of something good to eat) and then having its body touched by a human hand or brush. This is rubbed over all the most sensitive parts of its body – neck, withers, head, belly and finally tail – until it is ready to greet its handler with every sign of pleasure. At this stage, the tack can be placed on it (a head-collar on its head, a saddle on its back, and the girth gently tightened round its stomach), and it can be walked around carrying all this until its suspicions subside. Only at this stage – which may take several days to reach – will an experienced rider attempt to mount.

While carrying out all these processes, the trainer has to be aware of, and prepared to compensate for, all inborn or 'instinctive' fears that a horse may demonstrate. As mentioned earlier, all horses are born with a natural fear of any moving object approaching from front or rear. In addition, there are idiosyncratic fears that are peculiar to certain families, such as a desire to be dominant (and a dislike of being ordered about) or a tendency to be submissive (dependent on a leader whom it can trust). I once owned two mares, from each of whom I bred several foals. If confronted with a stranger or a new object, one of the mares would lay back her ears, turn her back on it and kick out as if to destroy it before it could harm her. The other would prick her ears and walk towards it enquiringly, then push it with her nose, and if it responded threateningly, strike out at it with a forefoot. The offspring of both mares followed their dams' behaviour patterns in detail, even if (to my knowledge in one case) the foal had never seen its dam behave like that.

I also found that all the members of the first mare's family (the kickers) liked the rider to take charge when being ridden and to act as their guide and mentor (i.e. the parent); whereas the others (the stampers) liked to think that they were the bosses and were only complying with my wishes out of politeness. So my advice to all those breaking in a young horse is to be prepared to vary their own approach to suit that of the horse.

To do this successfully, one should, if possible, study the horse one intends to break-in together with its companions before they are separated, to see if this horse is naturally a leader (a boss horse) or one of the followers. If it is a natural boss, it does not follow that its willpower has to be broken or its spirit tamed before its co-operation can be gained (as used to be imagined). Through tact and by showing a willingness to accommodate the horse's desires wherever possible, a human can establish an excellent relationship with such a horse (the sort that often leads to great achievements). In other words, by adopting an attitude that might be expressed as, 'All right! I'll leave it all to you, but let me show you where to go, and the best speed to do it at', the trainer establishes a partnership with the horse that does not wish to be dominated.

With horses that are natural herd followers, however, a completely different attitude has to be adopted: the sort that says, 'Come on! If you trust me and do as I tell you, nothing will hurt you.' Only if a rider lets his or her horse down by failing to look after it in the second example, or by failing to go along with it in the first, will the bond of friendship and confidence be broken – a tragedy that often takes a long time to overcome.

In addition to dominance and submission, there are certain family lines that have their own particular phobias. I once bought a mare and bred from her and in so doing discovered she had a phobia about having her head touched. When all the foals from this mare first felt anything on their heads and behind their ears, they would throw up their heads and rush backwards until they were cornered against a wall and could go no further. This fear took many months of careful and pains-taking daily comforting and cajoling to overcome, but even long after it had apparently been cured, it tended to return if anything unusual occurred in the vicinity.

Most trainers like to begin a horse's acclimatisation to the human presence as early in its life as possible. I have found that it is a great help to do this while the foal is still with its mother, so that she can be present to reassure her offspring and set it a good example. Her gentle whinny if it starts leaping away from an outstretched hand or rushing round behind her to hide, is very effective. Gradually, as and when it matures enough to carry one, a saddle can be placed on the foal's back (usually at two years old), and it can be led around to grow accustomed to the feel of the weight and the tightened girth. Even after this lengthy preparation, however, it may still be alarmed when a human first climbs onto its back; and it is as well at this moment to have someone on the ground at its head, talking to it reassuringly and possibly holding out a favourite morsel of food to encourage it to move its jaws and thus help it to relax.

When it is finally asked to take its first steps forward with a rider aboard, I like to have either a handler or another horse beside its head to reassure it; for if once it starts trying to buck or kick the rider off, this can quickly turn into a habit that may make the mounting process difficult for a long time.

Once a horse has learned to trust, and carry, a rider, it is possible to begin teaching it the rider's language, i.e. the 'aids'.

Most trainers like to begin a horse's acclimatisation to the human presence as early in its life as possible

These are usually given by touch – pressure with the legs on the horse's flanks to go forward, pressure on the lower jaw with the bit to slow down or stop – accompanying each correct response with a 'reward' (in the form of a vocal cooing phrase such as 'good boy', or a gentle pat) and each incorrect one with a growl or slap. Once a horse has confidence in its rider (and the rider has confidence in himself), it is amazing what dangers and difficulties they will survive together. I discovered this in the early post-war years, when I began riding one horse without the usual riding gear or aids, having developed an idea that horses might make better show jumpers if their heads were left entirely free, so as to balance themselves round corners and when altering speed or changing direction.

At about that time I had been involved in a study comparing the sensitivity of the skin over different parts of the horse's body and in horses of different coat colours, and it had become apparent that the neck in front and to the side of the withers – the area where, in fact, horses usually 'nibble' one another – was particularly sensitive to the touch of the human hand. It occurred to me that if signals had to be given by a rider on parts of the horse other than the sides of the mouth (by the bit) or on the flanks (by the leg), then a touch with the fingers on the sides of the withers might be the ideal method to try. A sharp backwards scrape with both hands could signal 'stop' or 'slow down', a sharp forward thrust could mean the opposite ('go' or 'faster'), and a push on either side could mean 'turn away'.

It did not take any longer for a horse to learn the meaning of these signals than it did for one to learn the conventional aids, even when simple flat work was combined with elementary jumping. But then came the all-important question of what would happen in a strange environment. Would the bitless horse be as controllable in public as a fully kitted one – or would the last anyone saw of me be a disappearing backside sinking over the horizon?

This is where I had my greatest surprise and satisfaction. In strange surroundings, my horse was *more alert* to my signals, *more obedient* to a command and *more amenable* to my desires than it had ever been at home. It seemed as though, whereas in its home territory it knew what to expect and what it could get away with, in strange surroundings *I* was its only link with security and it was on me that it depended for its safety.

In horses particularly, the tendency to associate a reward with the actual deed carried out by the horse before receiving it is common and leads to a repetition of the act. In fact, this is the basic method of training horses to do what one wants them to do. However, if shying at a roadside hazard, refusing to jump a ditch, or banging on a stable door is followed immediately and every time by a juicy piece of carrot or a reassuring pat on the neck, a horse may come to associate this prize with its undesirable behaviour, and so turn the initial act into a habit.

Mrs Gill Hawkins described one such case. Pia, her yearling filly, was used to being led across the farmyard, following her dam, to be put out in a paddock for the day, and then brought in at night. During some repair work on an adjacent road, it was necessary for the workmen to dig a ditch – about 60 cm (2 ft) wide – across the yard that the horses had always crossed. The first day she saw this hazard, Pia stared at it in amazement and refused to go near it despite being given a lead by her mother several times and being amply rewarded every time she looked at it. Eventually that day she did jump it, but on the second day, although accepting all the food and reassurances offered, she stubbornly refused to cross the ditch, and her owner eventually led her round it by a long, circuitous route.

This procedure was repeated on several days, until Mrs Hawkins's husband decided he had had enough. He armed himself with a large broom handle, and while Mrs Hawkins held Pia's leading-rein on the far side of the ditch, her husband administered a sharp whack on Pia's hindquarters. The filly leapt in the air in surprise – and found herself miraculously on the far side of the hazard. After she had been led to and fro over the ditch several times that day, with the broom always held menacingly in the background, Pia never hesitated at the ditch again.[3]

The main dangers to guard against in the early stages of training are:

1. Attempting to achieve more than a horse is physically and mentally capable of doing ('over-facing' it at an obstacle or continuing to work it when it is exhausted)
2. The trainer venting his or her own disappointment on the horse if it fails to achieve a task he or she has set it

Usually a light tap with a stick is enough to indicate to a horse that it has done something unacceptable, but there are times (as in the example just quoted) when a horse is clearly 'trying it on' to see what it can get away with, when more severe punishment *is* justified.

It is best, when starting to teach a horse a new task, to do so in surroundings that are familiar to it, and to use the same surroundings for all new lessons; in other words set up a 'schooling paddock' or area that a horse will quickly learn to associate with having to concentrate on what its rider is telling it to do. This is particularly valuable when teaching a horse to jump, for leaping over obstacles is not an activity it indulges in naturally. It is best to start teaching it this task by leading (or lungeing) it over a single pole lying on the ground and raising the height (and changing the position) of the pole gradually as the horse shows increasing awareness and acceptance of what it is expected to do.

By degrees, other types of obstacle can be added, but solid ones, such as brick walls, which cannot be seen through, are always likely to create most anxiety. A horse depends very strongly on its vision, and I once carried out several experiments to discover what sorts of things aroused its greatest suspicion. To my surprise, it was not so much the 'thing' itself that was important, but the 'thing' plus its surroundings, i.e. the 'total situation'. I explained this to Josephine Haworth, who quoted me in her book *The Horse-Masters* (1983) as saying,

> ... even the sight of a bale of hay put down where no bale had been before, was greeted with suspicion, particularly by the older horses who apparently have a more fixed image of what their surroundings *should* look like than the younger horses. A striped umbrella in the field was regarded as an outrage, although the same umbrella, seen being carried in the road, created no interest at all. A balloon placed in the stable yard where children's toys are often left lying about was looked on as commonplace, but the same balloon put into the horses' paddock caused snorting and stamping.[4]

A lead from a trusted equine friend in potentially frightening situations, such as over jumps or on busy roads, is the greatest help to a young horse. This again, is where a competent rider can be of the greatest assistance.

CHAPTER IX

Turning Fear into Fun

As has been stressed in the preceding pages, strong emotional sensations such as anger, disappointment and sorrow – and their opposites, joy and happiness – arouse much activity within the muscles and nerves. If not allowed expression, but 'bottled up', this emotion can cause severe pain, both at the moment of origin and at future dates when re-aroused by memories. However, giving vent to this excess of emotion – 'getting it out of the system' – can present a problem. Only too often humans show it in the form of verbal abuse directed at their spouse, next of kin or neighbours, while horses indulge in vices like kicking or crib-biting.

On the other hand, avoiding the arousal of strong emotions by doing nothing or lying around all day and night, does not result in happiness either. Life was designed to thrive on activity leading to further creation; on transforming the inanimate into the animate, on creating 'progress', or at least the potential for it. The living body cannot rest until a 'goal' is reached, and the emotions and activity assisting in this achievement are usually known as 'excitement'.

Games are of great assistance here, for they not only help to increase skills, but also provide jollifying distractions from any possible fears. Care has to be taken, however, to ensure that the activity aroused by the game does not interfere with the ability to perform the required skills. When newly enlisted soldiers were being trained to join the cavalry, a favourite way of teaching them to move with (as opposed to against) the action of the horse over a fence was to make them pull a stick out of the top of a fence as the horse went over it. This encouraged them to lean forward in the correct position for jumping, and so helped the seat as well as the nerve.

Attaining a goal is perhaps the secret of happiness, for it is only after such an attainment – whether the goal consists of winning a competition, climbing a mountain, creating a work of art, or merely accomplishing a routine job – that the individual can sit back, relax, and rebuild his or her body with a good meal.

Our use of horses in attaining goals goes back a long way. Horse racing has probably been indulged in for centuries, and there are records of polo being played in the Middle East since at least 3000 BC according to Harold Barclay.[1] Beating another individual (or individuals) to the goal adds to the feeling of success, and this is where organised competitions play such an important part in making leisure pleasurable.

The disappointment resulting from not achieving the goal can, however, be agonising, and can only be avoided if the goal itself is within possible reach. This is why competitions are most successful when organised in accordance with strict rules and regulations, so that novices can compete against novices, young against young, and champions against champions. Through competitions of this kind the opportunity for winning can be repeated and repeated until success *is* finally achieved or the desire to win fades.

In the last forty years, the need for non-harmful outlets for pent-up energy in both horses and humans has probably become more important than it has been for centuries. This is because the efforts made by most nations to replace battle against other nations with dialogue seem to be succeeding, and battles against the perils of nature are diminishing the world over. Instead of declaring war on other nations, we challenge them at sport. Instead of fighting against nature, we try to divert its forces into channels to feed us and provide us with warmth. Instead of having to go out and kill wild animals for food, we raise livestock on farms and disapprove of killing the world's wild animals.

This is not the first period in our history in which this seems to have occurred. When the classical Greek civilisation was at its peak it, too, faced the problem of re-directing human energy, and did so by means of games, culminating in the Olympic Games that were later resurrected in the twentieth century.

Horse-back riding provides the novice with a quite considerable challenge, as every beginner knows. The need to relieve a child's initial fear of riding through organised games and competitions has long been recognised by the British Pony

Horse-back riding provides the novice with a quite considerable challenge

Club, and its success in this respect has been acknowledged. Not only are competitions organised within each regional area, but areas now compete against one another.

It might be suggested that as only one person (or pair, or team) can win a competition, all the others may be left with a sense of bitter disappointment at the end of it? In other words, the organisers may be responsible for causing more bitterness and sadness than happiness. This is not necessarily always the case. Organisers have to be prepared to receive complaints of 'unfairness' and 'favouritism' from the unsuccessful contingent, but since they are very often former competitors themselves, they tend to know how these accusations originate. Today's competitors should always bear in mind that most organisers of equestrian sports work long hours in uncomfortable situations merely so that other people may enjoy themselves. Far from deserving criticism, they earn the gratitude of all competitors, and if disappointed entrants do not find other butts on which to vent their disappointment, they are liable to find themselves banned from taking part.

Many competitors overcome this snag by setting themselves their *own* targets (be it jumping a clear round, beating so-and-so, or just completing the course). Finishing first in the competition is not the only prize to be won. Putting up a good show, proving to yourself and your horse that you are as good as the rest, are triumphs in themselves and can be totally satisfying. As they say of the Olympic Games, it is the taking part, not the winning, that counts.

Indeed not all riders need to enter competitions in order to find satisfaction with horses. For many, a gentle hack along the roads is quite enough. For others, the ability to gallop across country is a sufficient challenge.

For a horse, having a human on its back for the first time is an introduction to a new world, and the way this initial training is done can affect its whole life thereafter. Many observers might doubt whether any horse can ever really *enjoy* some of the tasks it is asked to do in competitions. Can horses really get as great a thrill as their riders out of clearing a 1.8 m (6 ft) wall? Can they get pleasure out of galloping 6.4 km (4 miles) over the Grand National course? Are we not simply making slaves out of them by tying them up in dressage gear and making them 'dance to our tune'?

You would have to sit on top of a horse (or behind it in a carriage) and be able to feel or see its body language to be convinced that horses can derive as much satisfaction and fun from these challenges as their riders and handlers. Horses do need to let off steam, but how the release of this nervous energy can be turned into fun in the ridden or harnessed horse is another matter. There is probably no hard-and-fast method; every combination of horse and rider is unique.

It is not, of course, until a mutual partnership with a horse has been established that its co-operation can be enlisted for competitions. The essence of happiness and excitement for them, as for their riders, must be enjoyment, not pain. This is why the organisers of equestrian competitions insist that riders may use potentially pain-producing objects such as whips and spurs to 'signal' to their horses when an extra effort is needed (e.g. the winning-post is approaching or the next fence has a large ditch beyond it). However, 'misuse' of these aids to cause suffering is strictly forbidden.

One problem that has to be faced in all these challenges is that excitement (just like fear) can interfere with the performance of a well-practised task, taking the mind off a set routine and distracting the performer's attention. Another problem is that excitement in one animal (for instance another competitor's horse) readily infects others, hyping them up into states of agitation too. Even seeing the tackle associated with galloping across country is enough to distract some horses into paying less attention to their rider's immediate commands. To illustrate this, I will describe the life and progress of one of my own horses, Nicolette, who started performing in one-day events in 1987, under the care of Jeremy Bramham Law.

Nicolette (Nicki) is the fourth generation of a line I have been breeding since 1960, from a mare I bought in 1957, reputed to be by an Irish Draught stallion out of a Thoroughbred mare. Nicki's dam and grandam were selected for further breeding because of their ability and boldness across country, despite the fact that in their early years they had not been too easy to handle and had definite ideas of their own. They did not appreciate being ordered about, but were only too happy to share in the excitement of a rider, and both did well in local point-to-points.

Nicki's sire, Nickel King, belonged to an old friend of mine, and I had admired some of his stock for a long time before sending Nicki's dam to be covered by him. At the time Nicki was born, however, we had an extremely unpleasant, and possibly lethal, fungus on our land, which in Nicki's case caused large septic swellings to appear on her heels when she was one year old. The daily attention needed on these was objected to strongly but at least it enabled me to form a close relationship with my stroppy great baby, which stood us in good stead later. I have always made a point of handling my foals as much as possible from their first weeks of life, and have tried to make this pleasant and enjoyable for them by providing copious rewards. In Nicki's case, however, the handling was accompanied by painful washing and dressing of her heels, which rather offset the pleasure of the rewards, but eventually she came to tolerate the process and would even come up to me voluntarily when called for our evening sessions. There were plenty of other slightly older youngsters on the place at the time, with whom she played and frolicked out in the fields.

The following spring, Nicki's sore heels broke out again, and the swelling began to spread up to her hocks. By that time she had developed into a long-legged giant, who took considerable strength to control. This was not, however, the end of her childhood troubles, for when she was two years old she developed a very unpleasant nasal infection which made her cough badly and again necessitated traumatic veterinary attention. While all this was going on, I decided to take advantage of the situation and accustom her to a saddle and bridle, so that by the time we started to break her in as a three year old, she looked on the whole process as boringly harmless and put up no resistance at all.

Her natural athleticism made it easy for her to gallop and jump, and our only real problem came when we asked her to go over a shallow ditch for the first time. This required brute force (plus a lead from a friend) but once she had learned that her rider's judgement could be trusted and that he was not going to give in to her, jumping ditches presented no problems. In fact, Jeremy said:

My only problem in our early competitions was her apparent indifference to the whole thing. She lacked any desire to 'go forward' – or, in fact, go anywhere at all, being quite content to stand around and let the other horses do the prancing and jumping. My problem I suppose, was to develop this desire without excessive use of legs and artificial aids. The first thing we did was check her physical condition. This was found to be all right (except for an allergy to dust, which necessitated keeping her bedding very clean and soaking her hay before it was fed to her). The second thing I did was check the energy value of her feed. This was found to be low; so a high-energy diet was introduced over a period of three to four weeks. A notable difference could then be felt in all three phases. Dressage began to get a better rhythm and sparkle, and show jumping became more consistent as:

1. Her balance improved and so gave a more rhythmic and rounder stride
2. Impulsion around the arena could be felt
3. She developed the desire to clear the tops of the fences
4. She began to snap her legs up over the fences[2]

From the beginning, her performance across country had always been bold and obedient, though it had lacked rhythm and balance (only to be expected in a young horse). As her physical development and knowledge improved, so did her speed across country and her athletic ability over fences. Jeremy again:

> Her enthusiasm across country did produce one hiccough in her dressage. As soon as she began to anticipate her trip across country, her excitement began to make her fidgety in the dressage phase. This has been resolved by lungeing her for half an hour on arrival at the ground, and then riding her in for another half hour before the actual dressage test. To begin with, her fidgetiness may have been aggravated by the use of a special dressage saddle. Nicolette is such a tall horse that her back may not have been fully developed; and as one rides much deeper in a dressage saddle than in an ordinary one, it may have struck a weakness that an ordinary saddle misses. As soon as I changed to a jumping saddle for the dressage, her tension disappeared.[3]

In all cases, Jeremy stresses the absolute necessity for ensuring that all possible *physical* causes of pain should be removed (by making sure there are no leg troubles, back pains, or ill-fitting tack, etc.), before a horse is asked to do the tasks we set it, and second, that any possible fear of *rider*-imposed pain (from whips or spurs) is only used to overcome *object*-inspired fear (such as that of jumping ditches, complex combinations, drop-fences, etc.), and that even then it is brought into use in an easily avoidable way by starting off with small versions of the feared fence (which can be jumped from a standstill) and building up gradually to the required height. He also stresses the importance of the rider's mood, his own confidence in the task, and his desire to share all satisfaction and triumphs with his horse all along the line:

> This can brighten up a dull dressage test, encourage a laid-back show jumper, and tune up the cross country phase. A rider should never lose sight of the fact that he is the only one of the pair who knows what movements a dressage test involves, in which order the fences have to be jumped in the show jumping phase, and where the course goes across country. Unless he has developed (and keeps to) a system by which he can communicate the required

The rider is the only one of the pair who knows what movements a dressage test involves

moves to his horse in plenty of time for it to carry them out, there will be trouble.[4]

While Jeremy stresses the need to avoid over-excitement in competition horses and riders, as this might distract attention from the important tasks in hand, he feels that a certain amount of apprehension in a rider need not be a bad thing. It increases determination, makes the rider more positive in the way he gives the aids, and ensures that his horse goes well over the tops of its fences instead of brushing them with its feet. Over-confidence can result in sloppiness, and is just as great a hazard to achieving a goal as is its opposite emotion, nervousness.

Conclusion

The association between horse and man has a long history, and yet many of the complexities of both equine and human behaviour are still not fully understood.

Nervousness is a fairly common complication both to riding and being ridden, but it should not be considered an inevitable part of equestrianism, nor is it insurmountable.

The equestrian world is diverse. Different disciplines have different ways of coping with nervousness, as those involved with racing, showjumping or horse trials will know. In writing this book I have avoided too specific an approach, aiming the content at the everyday rider facing everyday problems.

Nervousness is a very individual experience. Conquering it involves three important stages

   i Recognising its existence
  ii Being prepared to deal with it
 iii Overcoming it

Bibliography

Ainslie, Tom; and Ledbetter, Bonnie (1974) *The Body Language of Horses*, Kaye and Ward

Argyle, Michael (1967) *The Psychology of Interpersonal Behaviour*, Penguin Books

Barclay, Harold B. (1980) *The Role of the Horse in Man's Culture*, J. A. Allen

Blake, Henry (1986) *Horse Wisdom*, Souvenir Press

Davies, J. A. (1988) *The Reins of Life*, J. A. Allen

Hartley Edwards, Elwyn (1987) *Horses: Their Role in the History of Man*, Collins

Haworth, Josephine (1983) *The Horse-Masters*, Methuen

Kazdin, Alan E. (1982) *Single-Case Research Designs*, Oxford University Press, N.Y.

Kiley-Worthington, Marthe (1987) *The Behaviour of Horses*, J. A. Allen

Larter, Chris and Jacklin, Tony (1987) *Transporting your Horse or Pony*, David and Charles

McBane, Susan (1987) *Behaviour Problems in Horses*, David and Charles

—— (1988) *The Horse and the Bit*, Crowood Press

Rees, Lucy (1984) *The Horse's Mind*, Stanley Paul

Schaeffer, Michael (1974) *The Language of the Horse*, Kaye and Ward

Waring, George (1983) *Horse Behaviour*, Noyes

Williams, Moyra (1976) *Horse Psychology*, J. A. Allen

Notes and References

CHAPTER I: *What is Nervousness?*

1. Diana Lister, *Equine Behaviour*, No. 18, p. 11.
2. Gillian Cooper, *Equine Behaviour*, No. 18, p. 13.
3. *Equine Behaviour*, No. 20, p. 19.
4. Bryan Jones, personal communication.
5. Sabrina Benson, personal communication.

CHAPTER II: *Inheritance*

1. Professor Vogel, *Horse and Hound*, July (1979).
2. Bernard Grzimek, *Z. Tierpsychology*, Vol. 6, p. 406 (1969).
3. Frank Ödberg. Thesis presented to the State University of Ghent (1969).
4. T. R. Roberts, *Equine Behaviour*, No. 19, p. 11.
5. Mary Good, *Equine Behaviour*, No. 20, p. 13.
6. Maurice Burton, *Phoenix Reborn*, Hutchinson, London (1959).
7. Sharon Cregier, *A Source Book of Farm Animal Ethology*, Captus Press Inc (1990).
8. Marion Boyle, *Equine Behaviour*, No. 3, p. 13.
9. Michael Osborn, *Equine Behaviour*, No. 5, p. 12.
10. Mrs Pegg, *Equine Behaviour*, No. 17, pp. 7–8.

CHAPTER III: *Growing Up*

1. Andrew Fraser, *Equine Behaviour*, No. 22.
2. Christine Belton, *Equine Behaviour*, No. 4, p. 16.
3. Janet MacDonald, ibid., p. 18.
4. Anne Eley, *Equine Behaviour*, No. 8, p. 20.
5. Veronica Snowden, *Equine Behaviour*, No. 10, pp. 10–11.

6. Anne James, *Equine Behaviour*, No. 14, pp. 16–17.
7. Joy Partridge, *Equine Behaviour*, No. 21, p. 7.
8. Mrs Dunn, ibid., p. 8.
9. Ibid., p. 9.
10. See bibliography: Schaeffer (1974); Ainslie and Ledbetter (1974); Rees (1984).
11. Gillian Cooper, *Equine Behaviour*, No. 17, p. 5.
12. Gillian McCarthy, *Equine Behaviour*, No. 20, p. 33.
13. John Watson. Talk given to the Society for Companion–Animal Studies, November (1988).

CHAPTER IV: *Maintaining Peace of Mind in Horses*

1. Joanne Jones, *Equine Behaviour*, No. 16, p. 10.
2. Mary Good, *Equine Behaviour*, No. 14, pp. 15–16.
3. Sabrina Benson, personal communication.
4. Diane Harvey, *Equine Behaviour*, No. 17, p. 9.
5. Babs Elsworth, *Equine Behaviour*, No. 20, p. 31.
6. Deborah Street. As reported in *Equine Behaviour*, No. 5 (1980).
7. Gillian Cooper, *Equine Behaviour*, No. 17.
8. Work at the State University of New York. As reported in the veterinary magazine *Equine Practice*.

CHAPTER V: *Calming the Nerves*

1. See bibliography: Williams (1976).
2. S. Marinier and A. Duncan, *Equine Behaviour*, No. 4, pp. 11–12.
3. Carol Yarwood, *Equine Behaviour*, No. 15, pp. 15–18.
4. Sheila Asker, *Equine Behaviour*, No. 21, p. 22.
5. Richard Shrake, *Equinews*, March, p. 9 (1989).

CHAPTER VI: *Teaching the Nervous Rider*

1. Sabrina Benson, personal communication.

CHAPTER VII: *Calming the Human Mind*

1. T. R. Roberts, *Equine Behaviour*, No. 19, p. 11.
2. See bibliography: Blake (1986).

3. E. Royds, *Equine Behaviour*, No. 1, p. 8.
4. E. Royds, personal communication.
5. See bibliography: Kazdin (1982).
6. See bibliography: Davies (1988).

CHAPTER VIII: *Establishing Co-operation between Horse and Rider*

1. See bibliography: Haworth (1983).
2. Author observation.
3. Gill Hawkins, *Equine Behaviour*, No. 22, p. 26.
4. See bibliography: Haworth (1983).

CHAPTER IX: *Turning Fear into Fun*

1. See bibliography: Barclay (1980).
2. Jeremy Bramham Law, personal communication.
3. Ibid.
4. Ibid.

Index